Academic Betrayal

The Bullying of a Graduate Student

Loren Mayshark

Copyright © 2017 by Loren Mayshark

All Rights Reserved

Published by Red Scorpion Press
www.redscorpionpress.com
P.O. Box 289
Bemus Point, New York 14712

This book is protected under the copyright laws of the United States of America. Any reproduction or unauthorized use of the material or artwork herein is prohibited without the express written consent of the author.

Contents

Introduction 9
Chapter I 15
Chapter II 35
Chapter III 45
Chapter IV 45
Chapter V 55
Chapter VI 65
Chapter VII 71
Chapter VIII 83
Chapter IX 103
Chapter X 115
Conclusion 123
Appendix 129

Dedication

To professors Lawson Bowling, Jack Salzman, Jose Renique, Tim Tomlinson, and the many other great teachers I have had, too numerous to name here. Thank you so much for your massive contributions. Also, to college and postgraduate students everywhere, who I hope will benefit from these words.

ACADEMIC BETRAYAL

Acknowledgments

I would like to thank my mother, who has stood by me throughout this process.

Thanks to my aunt Vivian, who read the manuscript several times.

Thanks to my aunt Mary and uncle Tony for advising and guiding me.

Thank you to my father for his support of my dream to teach and his encouragement to quit grad school because he thought it was "bullshit."

Thank you to all of the administrators, tenured professors, and other faculty at Hunter College who gave me so much grief that it inspired me to write this book.

Thanks to Nick Rizzo, for his helpful advice and delicious cooking.

A special thank you to all the brilliant and humane teachers and professors that I have had in my career who have stood out at various institutions, including Hunter.

Thank you to John "Rue" Danielski, the Danielski family, Matt "King Crab" Kantack, Dan "Dom" Dominick, Matt Curtis, the Sweeneys, James Hanks, and the many other people who put me up during my pursuit of the elusive master's degree.

Thank you to Cornelia for her support through my tortuous breakup with this college and for enduring the recounting of the agonizing details.

Thanks to my cousin Angel Lipari and my wonderful family in Italy, who gave me an opportunity to end my years of fruitless toil and experience brighter skies in Europe.

Thank you also to my sweet cousin Brie Lipari, who has always been supportive of my pursuits and shares my passion for history.

Thank you to Peggy Fitzgibbon, Melissa Bartok, Elizabeth Schmitz, Shannon Donovan, and the many other wonderful librarians I have known.

A special thank you to Casey Ellis for his editorial insights and support throughout this process. Without him the book would have never reached publication.

Thank you to all the great people at Red Scorpion Press for their encouragement.

Thanks to Keith Miller for his keen editorial suggestions.

Thank you to all other friends and family members, too numerous to name here.

Disclaimer

Lawyers and editors have advised me that it is unwise to use the actual names of the people involved in this saga. I have elected to change the names of the primary actors. In no way does this diminish the truth I have meticulously documented. I have done so because my extensive training in the field of history has taught me that a case is only as strong as the evidence. I have correspondence, official documents, and other pertinent pieces of evidence in my possession, but to publish them would be courting litigation. Therefore, I have simply cited and summarized them as much as possible since the parties in question have demonstrated that seeking permission would be a futile endeavor.

I have elected to use the real name of the institution that I attended because I feel it is my duty to expose their malfeasance in hopes that other people will not subject themselves to the injustice that I have experienced. What follows is a detailed and hopefully entertaining account of my academic career at Hunter College in New York City.

Introduction

Maybe you've heard some version of this "Life 101" lesson from a teacher, parent, or mentor: "You get out what you put in." Unfortunately, that isn't always the case. When I entered Hunter College as a nonmatriculated student in the fall semester of 2008, I was eager to begin their master's program in history because I wanted to be a college professor. I believed that teaching was the best way for me to find a career, using my unique abilities; it would allow me to positively affect the world. I believed that my place in life would be more fulfilling if I pursued this altruistic path.

Six years and tens of thousands of dollars later, I left Hunter without a degree. I attended the thirty-credit program continuously for more than half a decade, and paid for more than the thirty credits required for the degree. While in the program, I maintained better than a 3.6 GPA. And I walked away with nothing. My situation may seem extreme, but after extensive research and speaking to numerous people in higher education, I have come to the conclusion that my situation serves as a microcosm of what is happening to higher education in the United States.

My perspective has obviously been colored by my negative experiences at Hunter College. But my understanding of the broader picture of where higher education is headed in the United States has been influenced by reading numerous articles and speaking with countless people who work or have worked in higher education in the United States. Of these perspectives, perhaps the most important comes from Noam Chomsky, one of the premier public intellectuals in the world, who has spent more than fifty years at one of the most prestigious universities in the country, MIT.

When I read "How America's Great University System Is Getting Destroyed," which is a transcript of Chomsky's remarks to a gathering of the Adjunct Association of the United Steelworkers in Pittsburg, Pennsylvania, I was astonished by the parallels between his assessment of the trend toward the corporatization of education and the collateral ills of our education system (specifically higher education). Chomsky, who has spent nearly his whole life as a student or teacher, has seen the university system greatly altered during his tenure. He begins his discussion of the situation by explaining that the corporate business model is "designed to reduce labor cost and to increase labor servility."* This model works by pushing the costs onto the consumer, which in the case of higher education means the students. As Chomsky explains, this is part of a wider movement to separate the population into two groups: the "plutonomy" and the "precariat." The uberwealthy thrive upon the precarious position of the "precariat" workers, who are so insecure in their livelihoods that they will not dare to strike or ask for additional benefits because of the risk of weakening their position. This is intended so they will better serve their masters. Alan

---

* Noam Chomsky. "How America's Great University System Is Being Destroyed" (lecture, Adjunct Faculty Association of the United Steelworkers, Pittsburgh, PA, February 4, 2014). http://www.alternet.org/corporate-accountability-and-workplace/chomsky-how-americas-great-university-system-getting. Accessed January 1, 2017.

Greenspan considered this vital to a thriving economy because of the power it transfers into the hands of corporations. This is exactly what Hunter College and many institutions like it have instituted: a system that preys upon students.

Some colleges have become institutions that no longer thrive on education, but rather on the suffering, expense, toil, and insecurity of their students, as well as insecure faculty and staff. Most of the professors I enjoyed at Hunter were adjuncts. They were interesting professors and some of the finest educators at the institution. They were also the ones who expressed their distaste for aspects of Hunter and the people in charge of the department. So it is often not the people with a love of teaching and reverence for education who generally make it into positions of power at Hunter. It is people with the most guile, the career-oriented professionals, who reinforce the cold policies of their paymasters. As a result, everyone below the top tier suffers and so does the educational integrity of the institution. This was my experience at Hunter, and many people I have spoken with regarding other institutions have echoed this concern.

In his article, Chomsky reminds us of the conversations about education that took place during the Enlightenment and that continue to shape our education system today. Two major philosophies were considered: the vessel model and the string model. Much of our education system is based on the vessel model, where the content is analogous to a liquid (information) that is poured into the vessel (student), which takes in and returns the liquid. This is the underpinning of standardized testing, which has birthed philosophies and programs like "teach to the test," Race to the Top, and No Child Left Behind. Students are made to memorize material for a test, which often devolves into cramming for an exam—something we've all done from time to time, usually out of some combination of procrastination, indifference, and time constraints. This model seemed inefficient to me, and I started a dialogue with people in education about it.

When discussing the vessel model with friends who work in math and science education, I heard some viable arguments for standardized tests. However, the system is deeply flawed, and it has even less efficacy in the humanities. Vessel education is alluring to administrators because it allows them to account for the information in standardized tests to show that the educators under their supervision are falling in line. It generates statistics to more easily measure "success" and to secure funding. Most Enlightenment thinkers opposed the vessel model and favored the string model.

In the string model, the educational program lays out a structure to facilitate the goal of having the student "acquire the capacity to inquire, to create, to innovate, to challenge—that's education."* As a famous physicist says to his class when asked what he will cover during the semester, "It doesn't matter what we cover, it matters what you discover."† That is the heart of this style of education: inspiring students to see education as an exciting process of discovery rather than the drudgery of memorization, which inevitably sparks this question in the bored mind of the student (vessel): "When are we going to use this?"

In the string style of education, the start of the string is often a question. Chomsky uses the example of a high school science program that poses the provocative question: "How can a mosquito fly in the

---

* Ibid.

† Quoted in Chomsky, "How America's Great University System Is Being Destroyed."

rain?" He explains that if something the size of a raindrop in proportion to a mosquito would fall on you, it would at least ruin your day, if not kill you, so why doesn't the raindrop immediately crush the mosquito? To answer this question students are forced to delve into complex facets of biology, math, and physics. The questions transform learning into a process of discovery that ultimately compels students to become interested in discovering the answers. Bottom line: education in the United States has lost this process and is deteriorating in many ways.

Higher education should be at the cutting edge of research and progressive education. Too often it is not. Educators past the high school level are no longer beholden to state-mandated measures or assessments, yet there should be some measure of accountability for people at the college and postgraduate level. These institutions have become so powerful that the individuality of the student is often no longer important to some institutions. And they are funded by the tuition that students pay (along with taxes). Full-time faculty members at the college level generally earn much higher wages than primary and secondary educators. But paradoxically, as one moves up the levels of education, there is often less accountability and, in some cases, less interest in teaching and working with students.

Unfortunately, the problems in higher education are not limited to professors; the problems are part of a system that starts with our national attitude toward education in general. This disposition, when filtered through institutions of higher education such as Hunter College, cause great challenges for faculty working in the system. These problems ultimately trickle down to the students. Some of the major issues with higher education in the United States can be seen in the bureaucratic machinations of the institution.

The system of higher education in this nation must be reformed. My situation at Hunter was an extreme case, but one that will resonate with many current students and former students who have completed college and now seek graduate degrees. My story is a microcosm that elucidates many of the problems in our system that tragically go unspoken.

At Hunter, I was systematically beleaguered in my pursuit of a degree and a career. I had been a good undergraduate student and was encouraged to go to grad school by some of my professors. I took time to work and explore other avenues, including travel. Those experiences allowed me to determine what I wanted to pursue in school, and I entered grad school ready to do a great job. What follows is a chronological account of my entire experience with Hunter College.

Chapter I

My story begins at the end of my experience at Manhattanville College, a small liberal arts school in Westchester County, New York, which was a transformative experience and completely different from my experience at Hunter. I worked hard at Manhattanville and learned a great deal on my way to earning a 3.3 GPA (3.6 in my history courses). I had many wonderful professors who inspired me to learn and treated me with respect. When I left Manhattanville, after receiving a BA in history, I felt it had been one of the best periods of my life; I had learned a great deal, in and out of the classroom.

After college I had the opportunity to become a stockbroker. More than one recently graduated friend working on Wall Street had given me the "Hey buddy, look me up and I'll set you up with an internship (or job)" invitation. My stockbroker dream had taken hold at an early age when I found out that one could turn a profit on a hunch or tip. It was the same impulse that fed my fascination with horse racing, which started at about the same time—age fourteen or so. I bought fifty shares of Invitero Fertilization of America (IVFA) for $250, essentially the last of what was in my savings account. After a year of holding it, I eagerly cashed in, doubling my money, and after that I was off and trading. I would read *Barron's* and the *Wall Street Journal* weekly, and because I had invested during the dot com boom, I was able to hit some valuable stocks and make a few thousand dollars. At the end of high school, I liquidated my investments and spent the money on college-related expenses as I made my way through Manhattanville.

In college I found more interesting and exciting ways to spend my time than sitting at home and speculating on the stock market. By the time I graduated, the ideas that I had been exposed to made a life on Wall Street seem dull and futile. I eschewed the conventional path to fortune for the unpredictability of the open road. After a wild period of living the vagabond lifestyle following graduation, I moved to San Francisco in 2005 to start a new chapter.

The first day out of bartending school, one week after moving to the city, I was hired for a bartending position on the spot. I worked in the bar at the well-known Fisherman's Grotto #9 on Fisherman's Wharf. I knew no one in San Francisco, and I rented a cheap hotel by the week downtown. I would walk to and from work (a couple of miles up and down SF hills), so my job was essentially my social life until I moved into a share house a month later. At the restaurant, the majority of the staff members were Latino or Chinese. It was a huge bi-level building that could seat a couple of hundred guests. When I walked into the back of the rustic old building, many of the Chinese men would be yelling at one another in Chinese, chopping up fish, or huddled around the table together eating on their breaks. In the kitchen, when I went to pick up food, a mix of Chinese and Spanish was hurled back and forth behind the line, and English was only marbled in as a necessity. Some of the Mexican waiters looked out for me and became my friends. Upon learning that I had an interest in the language, several of them would indulge me by answering my questions about the language and engaging me in conversations in Spanish.

I had always been terrible at foreign languages. Though I was a good student in other subjects, I had opted out of my New York State Regents diploma (a higher degree than a run-of-the-mill diploma), simply because I did not want to take a third year of French. When I went to college, I had to take Italian and Spanish, which were my only two pass-fail classes. I took Spanish in my final semester, and I feared that I was going to fail and not be able to graduate. But my teacher was kind and compassionate about my lack of linguistic ability. Ultimately, she helped me pass the class. So, even after formal education in three foreign tongues, I was convinced that I had no capacity.

This did not change the fact that I'd always had a burning desire to learn another language. When I was young, my mother and many members of her family spoke Italian or Sicilian around me if they were speaking about something they didn't want me to understand or they were using an idiomatic expression that wasn't translatable. But I just couldn't pick up the language and eventually became embarrassed by this inadequacy.

After moving to San Francisco and meeting many multilingual people, I was determined to learn Spanish. I bought Berlitz's first-level Spanish course and was presented with a perfect opportunity to learn. I would sit up at night flipping flash cards and listening to CDs as I fell asleep. I would constantly drill myself with flash cards as I rode the bus to work. It was exciting; I was finally starting to learn! On occasion, the waiters were kind enough to take me, after work, to one of their favorite bars in the Mission District. None of the bartenders spoke English, and I was forced to use my Spanish the entire night. A couple of drinks always made it easier for me because I wouldn't censor myself or dwell on the proper grammar. As my relationships with my co-workers grew, I spent time at their houses and with their families, and I fell in love with the culture and the language. I was astounded by their work ethic and warm, welcoming nature. I sat with rapt attention, listening to my friends as they told me about their lives in Mexico. It was fascinating to hear why they ended up deciding to come to the United States, and I found their tales of making the trip to the north compelling.

Nora, my girlfriend at the time, worked with me at Fisherman's Grotto and shared my interest in Spanish and Latin American culture. Our passion inspired us to sell our possessions, save as much money as we could, and use our security deposit to buy tickets to South America so we could travel and study Spanish. After an amazing five-month trip through the southern portion of the continent, filled with learning and countless new experiences, we returned with a different sense of the world. Although I was not fluent, I could hold a conversation and take care of every facet of our trip in Spanish, from bus schedules to acquiring food. I was thrilled with my progress.

When we returned to the United States, instead of going back to San Francisco, we settled in my hometown. Nora campaigned for us both to go back to school. She felt that it was a good idea to have an occupation that provided healthcare and a pension so I would have the ability to provide not only for myself but a family one day. Then I would be able to tell my grandkids that they would be secure, without a system once called "social security." It seemed like a way to find purpose and earn a quasi-comfortable retirement after sixty-five. So I was persuaded that, now that I was in my mid-twenties and enduring a combination of ailments stemming from treating my body like it was indestructible for the previous decade, it might not be such a bad idea to get out of town and pursue a career in higher education.

I began my search for graduate school the same way I began my search for college, and for the same reason: I didn't know what to do with my life. Four years before, when I was a recent college graduate, I had signed up for the standardized test for graduate school, the GRE. I did not do well, I believe because I was ambivalent about the future. I had such a terrible time with the test that I refused to take it again. At that time in my life, I saw it as an annoying hoop to jump through, with little bearing on reality.

I selected eight schools: two schools in Beantown, Boston University and Boston College; three schools north of the border, the University of British Columbia, the University of Toronto, and McGill; the University of Iowa; the New School; and my "safe school," Hunter College. I'd studied history as an undergraduate, and my passion for the subject and newfound interest in Latin America seemed to make an MA in Latin American history the obvious choice. I applied to MA/PhD programs, which were offered at half of the schools. These programs allowed one to earn PhD credits while completing a master's in the same program so that at the end of five or six years I would receive a PhD for my troubles. I applied to master's programs in the remaining schools because I figured if I couldn't get into an MA/PhD program I could start by getting a master's degree and become an adjunct professor, which would allow me to gain some experience before committing to a PhD. Teaching and a dedication to learning are in my family, and I was overwhelmingly supported in this pursuit.

The application process was difficult. Throughout my academic career I was an above-average student who never paid acute attention to details. I especially hate doing repetitive paperwork, which inevitably deprived me of getting great grades. But I was a more mature applicant during the grad school application process. I was ready to do whatever it took to attain this degree. I would sit for hours, grit my teeth, and methodically fill in the answers to tedious questions like where I'd gone to grade school. The process was repetitive, with the same information required on every application. Then I had to contact three of my old college professors. One of them had helped me immensely over the course of my life, but I hadn't spoken to the other two in four years. I spent the better part of five months wrangling together all the necessary documents and qualifications. In total, I spent over $500 in processing fees ($125 of which went to Hunter College, which was the most expensive). Since I had made the commitment to return to school, I became excited by the prospect of reentering the classroom to challenge myself to learn new information and skills. I waited eagerly for the results... and then the first letter came in.

It was a letter of rejection from Boston University. Six letters of rejection would follow. Finally, one school said they would extend an invitation for me to take classes as a nonmatriculated student: Hunter College. I could have tried to move to one of the other schools to take a few classes and eventually get in, but it didn't make much financial sense. Essentially, my choice was made for me. Hunter did have some virtues that actually made me excited about the prospect of attending there. It had a solid reputation as the finest of the City University of New York (CUNY) schools, and as a New York state resident I would pay in-state tuition, which I figured would cost me in the neighborhood of $10,000 for my master's, almost unheard of in this era when a single year of college can cost more than $50,000.

Hunter's was only a thirty-credit program for an MA in history. Of the thirty credits, three would be my thesis; of the other twenty-seven, nine could be taken in other related disciplines. Also, nine could be taken outside the institution at another CUNY school. It seemed to me that Hunter was an institution that allowed the individual student some intellectual latitude, and for a freethinker like me that prospect was very appealing. I applied for the program in Latin American history. Nora was thrilled, because living in the city would allow her to be close to her friends and family, and she could possibly attend the Fashion Institute of Technology, which was a leading, and affordable, institution in her area of study.

In preparation, we moved to Southold on the east end of Long Island, in May 2008. I worked as a caddy, bartender, and vineyard worker to save money in preparation for beginning school and our eventual move into the city. I worked in the fields with the grapes, side by side with the vineyard's predominantly Guatemalan crew. With the exception of an intern who would occasionally show up, my boss and I were the only non-Latinos on the crew. I became deeply interested in the lives of the men I worked with. My work experience solidified my notion that I would write my master's thesis on Latino labor on the east end of Long Island, with hopes of eventually publishing it as a book.

At the same time, I was working on a novel. I was flattered that the manuscript had been requested by an editor of a major publishing house to be considered for publication, but I could no longer give it appropriate attention, since my three jobs greatly disturbed my sleep schedule. I felt like I was always exhausted and behind. For the first time in my life, I started to become an insomniac.

During this zombie period I enrolled in my first class, as a nonmatriculated student at Hunter, in the fall semester of 2008. The class was Democracy and Development in Africa and Latin America. It was on a Tuesday, and I would take the Hampton Jitney from Southold at 11 a.m. and would not return from Manhattan until 11 p.m. My life was changing and I was doing my best to adapt. I was shocked at how different graduate school was from my undergraduate experience, and how motivated I had become to do the work.

As an undergraduate, I sometimes would not cross campus for a class. But as a graduate student, I found myself traveling nearly five hours roundtrip for a single session. The class was taught by Professor Theodore Jefferson, who was an interesting man with a wealth of experience in international relations, including work at the UN. Having been out of school for four years, I worked hard to brush off the academic rust and was able to eke out a B in the class. It was one of the most difficult courses I had taken in my life up to that point. I knew that I was in for the most challenging feat of my academic career, but my relative success in the initial course at Hunter heartened me, propelling me forward.

A few classes into the first semester I met with graduate advisor Professor Hannah Wallace (at Hunter a single advisor in the history department handles all of the graduate students) to make sure I was doing everything I could to gain matriculation. She was a straightforward and obviously erudite woman. Although she was somewhat curt with me, her demeanor made me feel calm because she seemed to be well informed on Hunter policy. As I sat in her corner office amid a clutter of books, she told me, "If you receive a B or better, all of your credits will transfer into the program, and if you are doing everything correctly, I think you should not have a problem getting in." I breathed a sigh of relief, feeling the tension in my chest melting. I felt that I had little to worry about and that every grade of B or better would be transferred into the program when I was accepted as a fully matriculated student. The coursework was difficult, as I'd expected, but after the reassuring meeting with Professor Wallace, I thought that the administrative aspect would be simple. She made it seem that if I were to reapply after receiving such a grade it would only be a minor formality to enter the program.

At the appropriate time during the fall semester, I applied for full matriculation, but was denied on the grounds of low GRE scores, which seemed odd to me because I was already taking a class and proving that I could do the work. This was puzzling, but I still had two more classes to take before I would be maxed out on my nonmatriculated credits. I thought that my performance would have made the GRE scores irrelevant, but what could I do except continue on the path that I had started?

Students are allowed a maximum of nine nonmatriculated credits, and then the credits will not be taken into account in the program. So I signed up for two more classes for the spring semester: the History of Modern Mexico (the only grad course offered in Latin American history that semester) and History and Memory, a course that piqued my curiosity. One cannot sign up for any graduate courses without departmental permission. Professor Wallace granted me the permission to continue.

Meanwhile, Nora and I moved into Astoria, Queens, with her sister so we could immerse ourselves in our academic careers. Thankfully, I was within a half hour of Hunter by subway. The financial crisis of 2008 had just hit, so it was extremely difficult to get a job. Bartending positions were being filled by low-level traders who had lost their financial jobs in the economic downturn. I had to settle for a bartending job at a new wine bar in Queens that was nearly a forty-minute trip from our apartment. My employers proved to be shady and the job was ultimately hellacious, but that is a story for another time.

I applied to Hunter for full matriculation a second time while taking classes during that spring semester. The professors for both classes were brilliant and engaging, and demanded a great deal from their students. I worked hard in the classes and the semester was going fairly well. But in late April, two astonishing things happened: I had to quit my job because my bosses were stealing from me (and the other employees) and refused to compensate me fairly for the work I was doing. I was also diagnosed with spinal stenosis, and it was recommended that I get immediate surgery or risk becoming a quadriplegic. I elected to have emergency surgery in mid-April of 2009.

I found myself unemployed and, because of post-op complications, almost completely debilitated for more than a week. Moreover, I was in a Miami J neck brace twenty-four hours a day for the next four months. In spite of this, I strove to keep up with my coursework, even though I was offered an incomplete by both professors. I refused, assuring them I could finish. I spent hours propped up at my computer, wearing the neck brace, working to complete a lengthy paper, only stopping when the pain became unbearable. I only missed each class twice and handed in all of my work on time. I earned a B+ and A- in the classes, respectively.

I had a plan to take an independent study with the professor who taught my Mexican History class, which I worked hard to set in motion in the latter half of the spring semester. He was a brilliant and hardworking adjunct professor who had a passion for Latin American history. When I met with him with a full proposal for my independent study on the Latin American revolutionary spirit through literature, which I was extremely excited about, he became enthusiastic too. We checked with the department to see if I could do this independent study over the summer and, after some wrangling, the chair of the department, Professor Belview, said that he would allow it. But there was another catch: part-time faculty members were apparently not compensated for independent studies.

When the professor found out, he called me into his office and said, noticeably perturbed, "I can't do any more free work for these people." My heart sank and I told him how I felt that every time I had made some progress or got an interesting idea of how to get more Latin American history from their anemic curriculum (which offered one or two classes per semester) I encountered some sort of institutional barrier. I told him I thought that it was a flaw that a system would not allow an eager student and willing teacher to work on something that the student was prepared to pay for because of a "policy." He said that he understood my frustration and added that his daughter had gone to Hunter as an undergraduate but left in tears after a few semesters because the bureaucratic apparatus had chewed her up. Galvanized by the injustice, he told me he would take the project on for free, and I thanked him profusely.

However, I was once again denied matriculation. The only stated reason I could find was because of low GRE scores. I found this maddening, since I had already demonstrated that I could do an above-average job in my coursework. As a consequence of my denial of entrance, I was ineligible to take the independent study; also, I could not sign up for two more classes I was eyeing in the fall. I was only allowed to reapply for the program in the spring semester. I had been denied for the fall semester of 2009, which meant that I couldn't take any summer classes, including the aforementioned independent study. Bottom line: since I was maxed out on nonmatriculated classes, I could not resume taking classes until the spring semester of 2010.

I met with the chair of the history department, Professor Belview, about my problem with getting into the MA history program with a concentration in Latin America history. Belview was a serious sort of man who only used technical academic terms. He wore big, round bifocals with chic tan frames and dressed as if he shopped exclusively at Eddie Bauer and Land's End. He spoke slowly, in a measured and extremely serious tone. He was awkwardly tight and perpetually had the look of someone who had just finished pretending to laugh at a joke that a superior had made that he just didn't find funny. I wasn't sure he had the capacity to find humor in anything. I was very nervous while speaking to him, feeling I would make a grave error every time I opened my mouth. The tension grew by the minute.

I sat in his office, surrounded by books on ancient China and Southeast Asia, and looked out from the fifteenth floor of the Hunter west building, taking in the massive gleaming towers of New York City at midday and trying to calm myself.

"I don't think that GRE scores should be the only determining factor with regards to acceptance into this institution after an individual has proven that he can do the work," I said.

Professor Belview stared out his window at the high-rises and then fixed his gaze on me, which made me uncomfortable.

I nervously continued: "I have already paid for three classes in which I have a cumulative average of a B plus." I asked him if I could possibly take some independent studies that could count toward my degree and if he could allow me to take one more class while I was waiting for their decision. He said something dismissive, along the lines of "I understand your concern."

When I asked him why the history department only allowed graduate students three classes, and why they were frozen out and not allowed to take more classes until accepted, he told me that this was the way it was designed. Feeling desperate, I started to wonder aloud why it was set up this way, but he authoritatively cut me short. He told me that this was the policy and he could not change it to suit my individual needs. When he finished talking, it became uncomfortably obvious that it was time for me to leave. But I wasn't ready to depart, and I sat there thinking.

The policy strictly limited nonmatriculated students to three classes, but there must be some other way, I thought. The whole thing seemed painfully arbitrary. He mouthed something inaudible to himself, as if I wasn't there. Then he launched into his spiel about qualifications and how he didn't know how things worked until they reached his level. Essentially, he said that he couldn't help me get in any sooner. He told me to just apply again, and I should be able to make it. This was a constant theme: keep trying, keep paying, and somehow everything will eventually work out. I would have to wait to take more classes, with no guarantee that I would ever be accepted, much less be able to finish the degree.

The bureaucracy at Hunter was daunting and the staff was remarkably unhelpful. The experience I had with professors in the coursework was often rewarding and encouraging, but Hunter incorrectly stated that the program I was applying to actually existed, and no one ever told me otherwise the entire time I was applying to it and speaking with faculty. As a result, a serious problem developed that I was repeatedly assured could be worked out. My experiences systematically undermined my confidence, my mental well-being, and my finances. At this time I was unaware of what I would come to find, but getting matriculated into the MA program was my first major impediment.

Chapter II

My grand scheme to zip into Hunter and finish thirty credit hours in less than two years had vanished. Instead, I found myself in a neck brace and scrambling to rearrange my entire life. This ushered in a very dark period in which I often felt worthless. I took a Spanish class at the Brecht Forum and writing classes at the New York Writers Workshop and the Gotham Writers Workshop to hone the skills necessary to complete the degree. I applied to Hunter a fourth time (counting my initial application), and was finally accepted into the program. Since I was not eligible to take classes for the fall semester of 2009, I was charged an additional $125 to apply. The fact that I was being forced to pay the application fee twice to a program that I was accepted in as a nonmatriculated student seemed absurd. I started to feel indignant, so I wrote a letter in protest, but the reply came that it was "Hunter policy" and the fee would not be waived. It cost me a total of $250 just to get into the program. But at least I was in. I was convinced that my luck was shifting and the next semester would be a great one.

By the spring semester of 2010, I was finally out of my neck brace and relieved to be in the program. I was told by family members with master's degrees, professors inside Hunter, and other academic types I knew outside that once I was in the program everything would be easier. In the program I would have little to worry about, since I would have an exact path to navigate toward graduation. I scrambled to find the proper courses for that semester, which were filling up fast (since the MA program offered roughly seven classes total, in all concentrations, and usually one in Latin American history). I felt I was behind in this process and wanted to get into as many classes as possible so I could get to the thesis project I had dreamed about since working with the kind Latino laborers on Long Island.

I didn't find anything available in Latin American history, so I signed up for Modern Middle Eastern History, which I found very pertinent considering our nation's forays into the region. I also took a course on the Reformation wars, which had little congruency with Latin American history, but it seemed valuable to learn what was transpiring in Europe as the New World took shape, and I didn't have many other options. The third class was Historical Methods, with the jovial and gregarious Professor Gary Angelico, who was chair of the undergraduate department. Historical Methods was an extremely valuable class, and was geared toward understanding how history is recorded and how the historian can approach the craft of writing compelling historical accounts. The professor was wise, polished, and helpful, giving me more confidence in my situation at Hunter. He allowed me to tailor my course project toward an eventual thesis in Latino labor. For these classes I was granted departmental permission. Even though they fell outside the field of Latin American history, I assumed the classes were approved partially because students are allowed three classes outside of their concentration. The overriding reason the classes were approved was that they could not offer me an alternative in my field because they lacked the faculty. I was starting to discover that the department was actually not set up to support a degree in Latin American history.

It was at this time I made an observation about the courses offered, which I recorded in my journal:

SEPTEMBER 7, 2010

The department only offers eight to ten courses per semester, at best, and I am lucky if more than one of them is in Latin American history. And I can't just sign up for a class. Every class needs departmental permission, and one can't just show up to the registrar and register. It must be done online through a series of steps and from a couple of different passwords, an undertaking that is so complex that I still have not memorized it after a couple of years. Every single step through this bureaucratic tangle has been arduous.

To make matters worse, last night I found out that my tuition bill was due and must be paid immediately or I would lose my place in the classes that I need to graduate, which I had worked diligently to get into. When I went to administration a kind Indian kid with glasses told me that I had to speak with the bursar's office. When I walked over to the bursar's, it was closed at 1 p.m. on the Friday when my tuition was due, and I am sure I was not the only one frustrated by this. I returned to the admissions office and waited in line for the young man to tell me that the only other option was to pay online. I didn't have my log-in code with me, so I had to take the elevator to the student help center on the tenth floor in order to receive my password. Finally, with their help I was able to pay my bill, which took nearly every penny I had in my bank account and several hours. This was a complete surprise. Never before did I have to pay before the semester began to keep my seat. I was never notified, except for a message on the answering machine at my mother's house [which I found out about much later]. Additionally, I was hit with extra fees (as I have been nearly every semester because of their policy of closing registration for lengthy blackout periods, which is inexplicable since most transactions occur online), yet I was unable to receive a basic level of service.

Never in my four years at Manhattanville was there such a struggle to simply get into classes. There is a technological wall between me and every transaction I make at Hunter College. At Manhattanville I would pick my classes, write them on a piece of paper, get them approved by my advisor, and then walk down to the registrar to hand it in, and I was set. At Hunter I pick the classes, send an email, and await a reply to get approval from the history department. Then I have to go online and enter a code when the registration is not blacked out. Every time I have an issue I must wait in a line to see a registrar rep, who is usually rude and seems to have no power to work with the system. Invariably they send me to the computers in the hallway outside of the registrar's office so I can log on to make my changes that they should be able to do right there in front of me, face to face. And trying to call them is a dead end. After being on hold for a half hour during this process, I finally got through to a hostile woman. When I asked her for the course code I needed to register she grumbled that she didn't understand what I was looking for. After I explained my *situation again, the woman said, "I have no idea what you are talking about,"and then transferred me to the history department before I could reply. Hunter College is filled with rude and demeaning people, and it took me a while to understand that this is an attitude that begins with administration and trickles down throughout the entire system. I have encountered some kind and friendly people at Hunter, but from everything I have experienced, they are in the minority.*

Another time, I was simply told that I was ineligible to sign up for classes. In this instance I also called the registrar, because I couldn't just pop in to the college, and even if I did, I would be told to go outside and work with a computer rather than with one of their employees. If you call Oasis, the Hunter College registrar, you are put on hold and are told for a half hour by an automated recording how great Hunter College is. Then, when you finally get through, you are told that their department doesn't handle the issue. In this case it was problems with the health department, which was part of the reason I couldn't sign up for classes. I was then told that I had to contact the medical department for clearance. When I spoke to the health department they had no idea how I could become eligible for classes.

As it turns out, administrative problems are pervasive for Hunter students. I decided to look online for other students' experiences at Hunter, and one of the best resources I found was Yelp.com. There are, at the time of writing, ninety-five reviews for Hunter on Yelp, which give a net rating of 2.5 out of 5 stars. The vast majority of the positive responses are about the high caliber of professors at the institution or how "cool" and diverse the student body is. However, most of the reviews are negative, and say things like: "The administration is so rude it really is unreal" and "No communication between the offices" and "Kafka-esque monstrosity" and "This place has the WORST administration possible."

I could continue with reviews about how "The bathrooms are so filthy, you should get an STD test done ASAP" and other problems with the facilities, but that would be beleaguering the point. The bottom line is that the institution is riddled with problems. My case was extreme, but not without precedent.

Chapter III

Early in the spring semester of 2010 I met with my advisor, Professor Joshua Rosencrass, who had taken the place of Hannah Wallace as graduate advisor, in an attempt to find a tenable course of study to get my degree as soon as possible. At first he was unsure whether the institution even offered an MA in Latin American history. He tried to tell me that the Latin American history concentration in the MA history program simply did not exist. But I insisted that I had applied to this program and was accepted as a nonmatriculated student and later fully accepted into the MA program with a concentration in Latin American history. It was not until I directed him to the course catalogue on Hunter's website, as we sat together in his office, that he acknowledged that they did in fact have such a program. He gave me a befuddled look and said, "I guess it says they do offer Latin American history," and returned his attention to the computer screen. In common with several other programs at Hunter, there was no comprehensive exam offered for Latin American history, which at that time meant earning a degree in Latin American history was impossible unless an exam was written specifically for the student. I expressed my concern that the college did not offer many courses in

Latin American history, but Professor Rosencrass assured me that if I continued in the program, there would be greater opportunity for Latin American studies, because they were in the process of bringing in an esteemed professor from Columbia University, Molly Regresso, who specialized in Latin American history. He assured me that she would solidly anchor the program at Hunter. He said that he would accept my slate of classes as "an approved course of study" as long as I made my best effort to look within and outside the institution (at the other CUNY schools) for appropriate classes to finish my degree. I heartily agreed to make my best effort, elated that I was finally on the right track toward graduation.

In the meantime, he advised me to contact Professor Regresso, who was on a sabbatical and would not be at Hunter until the fall semester of 2010. He believed that she could aid me in the creation of the comprehensive exam in Latin American history. He was admitting that no such exam existed. Regardless, the course catalogue advertised degrees in "Latin American, African, Middle Eastern, East Asian, Jewish History..." in which the student is required to pass an examination in the specific field of study.* But when I had inquired about the Latin American exam, I was informed that the US and European exams were the only ones available for the MA in history. Professor Rosencrass believed that if I could develop a rapport with Professor Regresso, she would not only design an exam but could possibly advise my thesis. She sounded like the perfect solution to all of the problems that stood between the degree and me. My despair was replaced with hope.

---

* "The History Department at Hunter College offers courses in the history of the United States, the ancient world, medieval and modern Europe, Russia, Jewish studies, the Middle East and Islamic world, Latin America, Africa, East Asia and South Asia..." from the Hunter College of the City University of New York Graduate Catalog 2006–2009. http://www.hunter.cuny.edu/history. Accessed February 17, 2017.

At the suggestion of Professor Rosencrass, I began a protracted email correspondence with Professor Regresso. In the correspondence we discussed my situation and she encouraged me to sign up for her lone graduate history class in the fall, Colonial Latin America. She was unable to meet with me before the semester, but she assured me that we would be able to meet as soon as the semester commenced. No one would be available to help me before then. In addition to Professor Regresso's Colonial Latin America, I signed up to take two more classes in the fall, which would give me the magical total of nine needed to fulfill the coursework requirement of my degree: Modern Intellectual History and the History of US/Latin American Relations, which I took at Lehman College with the brilliant Professor Rodriguez.

At that time I was forced to move out of the city because my relationship with Nora was deteriorating and my financial situation had become dire. I moved in with an old college friend near Derby, Connecticut. This meant that my commute to Hunter was over two hours each way via train, and my trip to Lehman College in the Bronx took me about three hours each way.

It was during my class at Lehman that I had my first experience with CUNY's e-permit program, which allows students to take a course at another institution and have that course count toward the program in which they are enrolled. This was my lone experience with an e-permit:

OCTOBER 28, 2010

I'm now having trouble with my e-permit at Hunter, which is required in order to take a class at another CUNY school. My professor doesn't have me on the roster for the class at Lehman College even though I have signed up and paid for it. After listening to the typical automated Hunter bullshit for half an hour I was finally able to speak with a woman, who was rude and condescending. After I had partially explained my problem she interrupted me with some quasi-coherent rant, which only left me slightly less confused. When I asked her to clarify, she replied, "What did I just tell you?!" I wanted to say that it was a bunch of incoherent drivel, but I knew that would result in a screaming match so I gritted my teeth and then I told her that I was sorry and did not understand. She said she could not help me. So I called Lehman and was transferred to the one person who handles this esoteric e-permit system, and she was unavailable; she was out to lunch. When I finally reached her, she dismissively said, "You'll have to see if they still will let you take the course." I am furious because I had been commuting to the Bronx to attend this class for weeks. By this time one would think that I would be desensitized to this brand of inane screw-up followed by a salty demi-bureaucrat castigating me. But every time I feel like the storm of bureaucratic torture will end, there is a turn for the worse.

NOVEMBER 29, 2010

This is my third time returning to Lehman to pursue my registration for the e-permit. I played telephone tag with Tammy Whitman, Lehman graduate advisor, whose signature was my mission during the last attempt at solving my e-permit problem. She told me that it is not her responsibility to sign and referred me to Amy MacDonald, who she says is in charge of e-permits. I explained my situation to MacDonald's secretary and she told me to wait as she looked at the various documents: my letter from the professor, signed by the dean; my receipt of payment; email from Hunter for the class, etc. I was told again that it isn't her responsibility and I was told to return to Tammy Whitman, who was still on Thanksgiving vacation (it's Monday). Dead end. I returned to the registrar, who informed me that I could still register if I could get a more recently dated signature from the dean. "Why has it taken you so long?" said this fleshy, middle-aged, bleach-blond woman with glasses. I tried to explain that it takes me nearly three hours to get to the Bronx by train from Connecticut, but she cut me off with a wave of her hand and assured me that if I saw the bursar and updated the dean's signature she could probably register me. As I sat in the office of the dean, who was in a meeting for what had been a half hour already, the four women who work in the office crowded around the secretary as one of the other women took a picture with her cell phone. They were doing nothing work related. As I watched them I estimated that I had already put a minimum of twenty hours into this e-permit and I had yet to be registered for a class which I believed that I had registered for more than a month ago and have been attending since August.

After forty-five minutes I returned to the registrar with another piece of paper the dean's office gave me, which needed "notification" in the bursar's office, located in the basement. When I reached the bursar's office I found a line that went out the door and began to bend around the corner. After standing in line for nearly an hour, I was told by some automated machine to proceed to the next vacant window. I was beckoned by a hefty woman with a Caribbean accent who was sitting behind thick, bulletproof glass. She was curt, and as I handed her the paperwork I could not help but notice that she was dripping in gold necklaces, in her ears were giant golden hoop earrings, and on her wrists was an assortment of gold bracelets and watches. After I gave her my social security number she began to process the paperwork. As she processed, she sang along to a dancing mechanical pine tree on her desk which played "Rockin' around the Christmas Tree." When she finished, she told me that I was officially on the roster. I let out a relieved but exhausted sigh. After three months, I had finally gotten the e-permit.

It was almost as if they were intentionally trying to cause me to suffer and ensure I had a difficult time attaining my degree. I was starting to understand that behind everything I did there was a revenue source for the college, and I was running out of money. In an attempt to earn some money during this tumultuous period I started selling books on the streets of Manhattan on days that I had class, which would often lead to exhausting marathon days when I was up before 6 a.m. and did not get home until after 11 p.m. From the beginning of the semester the three classes I was taking were demanding and my unique work schedule, combined with my commute, created a situation where I was forced to read and write nearly every waking moment. I struggled to keep pace and was constantly exhausted. Here is a little note I wrote to myself one day while waiting for customers:

We are "programmed" from a young age not to quit and never to fail. But part of me feels that I have stayed with some bad situations too long because I wasn't going to give up. It seems that at this point I am only continuing because I feel I have passed the point of no return, with too much to lose after I have invested so much.

[Looking back on it, I wished I had found this quote, that day, from one of my favorite authors, Herman Hesse: "Some of us think holding on makes us strong; but sometimes it is letting go."]

After the first couple of classes in that semester I arranged a meeting with Professor Regresso to discuss my future at Hunter. Professor Regresso told me that she was sympathetic to my situation and was unsure why they would have accepted me as a student in Latin American history without adequate faculty to offer the requisite classes to prepare me for a comprehensive exam in the subject. I told her that this was beyond my comprehension, and it was a reality that was slowly coming to light for me. But I insisted that after investing so much time and money I had to finish. She explained that she would not feel comfortable endorsing my degree in Latin American history and putting her credentials on the line without me being properly prepared. I found that statement shocking, but did my best to conceal my surprise. She was more concerned about her credentials than my education.

In our email correspondence she had asserted that since Hunter did not require candidates to state their field of study in the application I could not assume there was a comprehensive exam in the field of Latin American history. I remember thinking that this woman had already become an expert on Hunter policy in her first semester at the college. She would fit in well here. I understood her point, but found it dubious that the course catalogue clearly stated that "The student is required to pass an examination in one field of history chosen from the following: ancient, medieval, early modern (to 1815), modern Western European (from 1789), British, Eastern European, American, Latin American, Jewish, East Asian, African, or Middle Eastern history."* This feat was to be completed in conjunction with the other degree requirements. Therefore, I had applied and continued to apply to the school for a program of study that did not actually exist. The entire time I had worked with my advisors, they never told me that I couldn't get a degree in Latin American history. I was being told this by a new member of the faculty.

This meeting took place after my first couple of classes with Professor Regresso and she didn't know me as a student. She would not make up a Latin American history comprehensive exam for me without my having taken a series of courses that she listed, but that Hunter College didn't offer. I told her that I couldn't take the US exam, which she essentially suggested, and I wondered aloud why she wouldn't be able to make a booklist for me to study in preparation for a Latin American history exam. She responded by pointing out that the US comprehensive exam covers four hundred years of a single country and that Latin America is a region with more than twenty countries, each with a unique history spanning more than five hundred years of recorded history. This, I must concede, was a good point. Why didn't Hunter consider this? I wondered. She said that it would be difficult to offer a Latin American history degree with a single professor as full-time faculty, which Hunter had not had since I applied to the program in 2008. At this point I realized that at Hunter everyone had a piece of

---

* Ibid.

the answer I sought but no one had the entire answer.

I was starting to wonder if it was my fault that I had not done more thorough research on Hunter's program. However, in my wildest imagination I could not understand being accepted into a program that I had continually applied to at an institution that claimed in their course catalogue to offer a degree in Latin American history, yet did not have the academic infrastructure to actually allow a student to complete that degree. The fact was that I needed to pass a comprehensive exam (in addition to the one I had passed in Spanish) and write a thesis. As I left Professor Regresso's office, I realized that I was in the final semester of coursework without a plan for a comprehensive exam or an advisor for the thesis.

I had done preliminary work for my thesis in the Historical Methods class and was passionate about the topic. All I needed was an advisor for the project. After consulting one another, Professor Regresso and Professor Rosencrass concluded that Professor Regresso was not the right person to help me, so they suggested I consult another new member of the Hunter faculty, Eduardo Caraja. Professor Caraja had joined Hunter from the University of Houston to anchor their history program in Latino histories. According to the Hunter website, he also has an interest in US political history and the burgeoning field of the history of sexuality. Since he was new, he had never offered a graduate class in a semester when I was eligible to take one, making us unknown entities to each other. I had an email exchange with Professor Caraja but was not able to meet with him until the second half of the semester. If he were to write a comprehensive exam for me it would be in the field of US Latino labor history, which would be a perfect precursor to my thesis on Latino migrant labor on the east end of Long Island.

Eduardo Caraja was my lifeline to a degree, and I was rapidly running out of options. When I walked into his corner office I was immediately struck by the man who sat across from me. He was slender and appeared young for a professor, maybe in his mid-thirties. A wisp of white cut through the front of his tightly cropped hair and made me think of a skunk. He sported a tightly groomed goatee on his serious face, and he spoke carefully and with a slight lisp. I remember feeling uneasy around him. He informed me that he would prepare an exam for me but would not commit to overseeing my thesis. I was initially disheartened by the fact that he would not commit to a thesis, but I didn't betray the brief disappointment to him because I was focused on the matter at hand, which was the comprehensive exam. He told me that he would send me a comprehensive booklist related to the history of Latino labor in the United States. Once again, the end of this fiasco at Hunter College seemed at hand, but at the same time I knew that I would have to expend a tremendous amount of effort to obtain the degree.

Chapter IV

After my meeting with Professor Caraja, I resolved to work harder through the semester so that I could finish the bulk of my coursework and be able to begin the booklist. I would have to digest the list as best I could and then regurgitate it in my comprehensive exam. I vowed to start reading furiously as soon as I received the list. Each of my classes inundated me with as much material as a human being could possibly force inside. The three classes I was taking required the reading of at least fifteen books—around five thousand pages of dense material in each class—and all of them included writing assignments, totaling at least twenty pages of carefully thought out term papers per class. Studying and keeping up with the administrative minutiae, combined with my bookselling and commute, made it nearly impossible to work and sleep. Once again I became an insomniac. Moreover, a mind like mine does not like to taste something interesting and move on; I am compelled to delve in further. This contributed to a painful internal struggle: wanting to take time to digest the information and do side reading, but barely having enough time to keep up. In graduate school there is no time to linger on interesting information or to be introspective, because one is so busy trying to pay the rent and cramming one's head full of information out of fear of failure.

On December 14, 2010, I received the booklist for Professor Caraja's custom exam. The list was a daunting thirty-eight books, comprised mostly of dry academic monographs. By that time I was wrapping up my final papers of the semester, which devoured every free moment. The day after the semester ended I began on the booklist. I read day and night, only taking breaks for utter necessities. I was operating on an academic level that I never could have conceived of before grad school. I was also exhausted and frequently depressed.

As part of my preparation, I had a series of meetings with Professor Caraja, the first of which was on January 5, 2011. I had subsequent meetings on February 1, February 14, and February 23. Each meeting lasted about an hour. In the meetings he was stern and serious, constantly challenging me to do more. I was very appreciative that he took the time to work with me, as I saw our arrangement as the last possible avenue to gain the degree that I had worked so hard for. I tried to convey my appreciation to him in person and through email; he would reply that he was simply doing his job. On several occasions he asked me if I felt comfortable taking the test in February and I told him that I wanted the experience of taking the exam to make me stronger and to push me, even if I did end up failing. Rosencrass and Caraja said that they respected my initiative and they would allow me to take the test, but they were skeptical that any human being could read thirty-eight books in roughly two and a half months. I was unfazed. The next test would not be offered again until September 2011, and as I saw it I was gaining valuable experience by taking the test in February. By creating the deadline I was disciplining myself to expend my maximum effort to finish the booklist. If I were to pass the test on the first try, great—then I could turn all of my attention to the thesis that I was so passionate about. Otherwise, I figured that the failed exam would make me much more prepared for the test in September.

I was in the process of moving out of Connecticut and back home to western New York State for financial reasons. This meant that I would have to commute four hundred miles for our meetings and the subsequent exam. I changed the setting of my thesis on Latino labor from the east end of Long Island to western New York, which Professor Caraja said would work fine if he were to take it on.

Over the course of our meetings I felt that I had built a mild rapport with Professor Caraja. Although he was always perfunctory, it seemed that his demeanor toward me was slowly softening. In the second-to-last meeting before the test he told me that he would take on my thesis as long as I understood that he would be on sabbatical in the fall of 2011 and could offer me no help from May 21, 2011, until the first draft of my thesis was due at the beginning of spring semester 2012. I was elated by the news and thanked him profusely, but almost immediately after leaving his office I refocused my efforts on the test.

A few days before the test, I returned to New York for my final meeting with Professor Caraja. Then I headed to my friend's house in Connecticut, where I spent the next few days cramming for the exam. The night before the test I writhed around in bed, riddled with a mix of fear, anticipation, and uncertainty. I was still battling with insomnia. I had to catch a ride to the Bridgeport, Connecticut, station to get the 7 a.m. train, which meant getting up at 5 a.m. for the test, which started at 10. One by one I swallowed the last few pills in a bottle of a natural sleep aid because I couldn't sleep. I popped one before bed, but

I just wrestled around in anticipation, so I repeatedly got up and popped another. Eventually, at 4 in the morning, I gave this practice up and just tried breathing exercises. I fell asleep just before my alarm went off. I tried to catch a bit of sleep by nodding off on the train in between looking at some study sheets I had prepared.

When I got to Hunter I was exhausted and felt terrible about the situation. I studied for a while in the lobby, and just before the test I bought a large coffee (I am very sensitive to caffeine) and sat down. Once the buzz kicked in, I flew through the test, writing down everything I could think of as fast as it came to me. The test consisted of three essay questions, each lasting one hour. Here is one of the questions: "Consider the role of Mexican-origin workers in the economic development of the Southwest. Why did Mexican-origin labor prove so pivotal to the growth and expansion of Southwestern industries and economies?"

I had to weigh the arguments of scholars against each other and provide an answer that demonstrated I was proficient in the historical data necessary. When I finished the test I was simply thrilled to have it over with, and I had a surprisingly good feeling that I had done better than I had expected, despite the challenges. I spent the night celebrating, and then I returned home and went to work on my fifteen-page thesis proposal, which Professor Caraja had requested by April 25. He would address the thesis proposal when I went to New York to go over the test with him.

Caraja was the primary reader of my exam, and mine was the only one he ever administered at Hunter. Everyone else in the room during the test was taking US or European MA history exams or the social studies certification exam, which was apparently easier. Caraja would read my exam and then pass it on to a second reader who would give input, but he would have the final say: pass or fail. I anticipated the answer for a month, trying to wipe it out of my mind, but it was always hovering over me. Finally, I was informed in an email from Professor Rosencrass that I had failed and would have to retake the test.

I was disappointed, but I figured that it was a realistic possibility that I would fail with such a short time to prepare. Having read nearly all of the books, I felt that the experience would give me a solid base to build from as I prepared to retake the test on September 24, 2011. Moreover, the books would give me a sound basis for the historiography section in my thesis and had given me a broad foundation of knowledge to guide my thesis. Although I was worn out and a little disheartened, after a short break I immersed myself in research for my thesis and began preparing my proposal. I sent him the full proposal on April 25. He told me that we would discuss it at our meeting in early May.

Finding professors to work with had been difficult, and dealing with the disappointment of failing the exam added some frustration. To make matters worse, I had to get permission to register for the one-credit class that I needed to keep my matriculation and to retake the exam; because they dragged their feet for so long before telling me I'd failed the exam, I had to pay an additional late fee. It was a simple registration of a one-credit course, which should have taken five minutes. It dragged on for months, causing me to spend valuable hours away from my studies writing emails, calling the registrar, contacting the history department, and so on. It put undue stress on me, which made me angry. When dealing with these inane tasks and the unfriendly people at Hunter, all of the frustration had the ultimate effect of sapping my motivation. When I finally had the opportunity to pay the tuition for the one-credit class to maintain my matriculation, it was $215, but then they fee you to death. The total after fees was $317.85, plus an additional charge of 2.65 percent for using a credit card.

In May I again traveled over four hundred miles in order to speak with Professor Caraja about both my thesis and my exam. Professor Caraja's corner office has a striking view that looks out into the Upper East Side of Manhattan. Pigeons fly as people scurry around fifteen stories below, like ants tending to unknown tasks. The first thing Professor Caraja told me was that he was so busy that he could only meet with me for forty-five minutes, and that he had no other time to meet with me for the rest of the week while I was in New York. I was astonished as he was telling me this, growing more shocked as I listed the days.

"Tomorrow?" I asked.

"No," he replied.

"Wednesday?"

"No."

"Thursday?"

"No—I just don't have the time to meet with you," he said with finality.

He then informed me that he would not be able to meet with me before the following January as he would be on sabbatical for the summer and fall. So, outside of a forty-five-minute window in mid-May, I would have zero time to review my test with him before the retake in September. He agreed that he would glance at some pages of my thesis if I sent him anything before May 21, but then he would be completely uninvolved with the paper until late January or early February of 2012. He chided me, saying that I was at a disadvantage for choosing an unorthodox course of study, and reminded me that it is difficult to work with a professor without taking a class from him. I agreed that I would have probably enjoyed taking a class from him and would have benefited from the experience, but since he hadn't taught a graduate class at the school until after I had taken the entirety of my courses this was impossible. So, after the preliminary discussion on his unavailability, I had thirty-five minutes to go over my thesis and another ten minutes to go over my three-hour test, which I had spent months studying for. The entire session felt dizzyingly rushed.

First, I was told that I had failed my exam because my introductory paragraphs were not specific enough and I couldn't sustain my arguments. Then he attacked the technical nature of my writing and said that he expected more from a graduate student. When I pressed him for examples, he pointed out a couple of two-sentence paragraphs, which he said were completely unacceptable at the graduate level. During his explanation he implied that I had slipped through the program until meeting someone with his serious academic prowess. I responded by telling him that I was not trying to make excuses, but I was given only an hour to develop these essays so I could only push forward as fast as possible, which left no time to revise. How is one to change the paragraphing in a timed, handwritten essay? I was simply dumping out the information from the thirty-eight books I had crammed in my head the best I could. I didn't have time for anything else during the exam session. I couldn't have gone through the test with a bottle of whiteout and fixed my paragraphs—it was completely unrealistic.

Looking at the test, all things considered, I thought I had done pretty well. There was nothing about it, aside from their opinion of my work, that made me feel like I was a failure. But as I inquired about the methods of their evaluation he became incensed. He could not tell me what the grading criteria was. This was perhaps understandable, since he had never administered this test before, but apparently this is something that he struggles with on his own exams. As one of his students observed on www.ratemyprofessors.com, he "isn't clear about how the grading is being done and when it comes to the exams, which are essays, you have to be VERY specific. Wouldn't recommend at all."

When I gave him a puzzled look as I was trying to understand why I had failed this exam, he coldly replied that his standards are "extremely high" and again alluded to the fact that we hadn't worked together, and added that if I didn't want to continue with him he would understand. I knew that there was no other person in the entire program who could oversee my thesis or exam, so it would be impossible to work with anyone else. I was trapped. I told him that I would work harder and show him a better effort on my thesis and on the next test.

After we'd discussed my thesis and the reasons I had failed the exam, I was told that I could look over my test but could not remove my exam from his sight due to "Hunter policy." He then told me that I was to stand outside his office while he locked the door behind him and went to the bathroom. I felt like I was in grade school as I stood out in the hall waiting for my teacher to come back, because he didn't trust that I wouldn't touch anything. When he returned I was given the exam, five full blue booklets in all. I hurriedly jotted down as many notes as possible. After about five minutes he told me that he had a "meeting with the department chair in ten minutes." When I began to tell him that I was still going over the test he told me that I had already taken more than an hour of his time. So I shut my mouth, knowing that the clock was ticking and arguing would get me nowhere. I wrote down as many notes as I could, but before I knew it my time was up and I was only beginning to review my second essay. As I walked into the elevator I felt cheated and insignificant. I began to worry, knowing that I would have to prepare for the exam again with very little feedback on how I was to improve my work. It felt worse knowing that the only person who could instruct me would be unreachable. I felt completely alone and vulnerable, unsure how I was supposed to proceed.

I had begun to notice a pattern. Every time I ran up against these institutional barriers or problems the onus was always put on me, never on the institution or faculty. My entire time at Hunter I had to either bend over and take it or walk away with nothing to show for my efforts. My time there was continually dragged out as I was treated like a child, while they attempted to explain away the results of their institutional limitations. At Hunter there was a cold competitiveness and an apathy that was palpable in many of the students and the majority of the professors.

Chapter V

After doing some research, I found out that this had been part of the culture long before I enrolled at Hunter College. The most extreme case I found about Hunter coldly putting the burden on the students was egregious but not surprising. In 2004 there was a young woman studying at Hunter who was suffering from mental illness, which I can imagine was at least exacerbated by attending Hunter College and dealing with their policies. She was admitted to the hospital after taking an inordinate number of Tylenol pills in a suicide attempt. Hunter policy on suicide at the time stated that a student must vacate the dorms and remain away from the school entirely for at least one full semester following the semester in which the student was banned. Additionally, "students with psychological issues may be mandated by the Office of Residence Life to receive counseling."

The young woman was professionally evaluated and found to not be a danger to herself or others. When she pleaded with the administration to let her stay they told her that she would have to leave. It was "Hunter policy." She returned to her room to find the locks changed. She was forced to pack up her room while being monitored by a security guard. This made a spectacle that worsened the situation, and one of her lawyers stated, "It was very difficult for her," because "she felt that everyone knew her business and was very uncomfortable."* Court documents revealed that the embarrassment she experienced once again plunged her into a depression that made her feel unstable. Even though she sued the college, Hunter still defended its policy in court until after settlement, when they promised to review the policy.

As a graduate student I did not have to endure the difficulties of Hunter dorm life on top of my administrative woes. But even dealing with many different professors with multiple agendas was trying. Hunter College raised the stress level for nearly everyone in the system, and Professor Caraja was purposely making it more stressful for me than it needed to be. I believe that the unnecessary pressure retarded my progress because humans don't always think clearly while under constant pressure for an extended period of time. Many bureaucratic problems and nonacademic stresses at Hunter made my learning experience more difficult than it should have been.

After my trip to NYC to meet with Caraja, I returned home dejected. I spent a couple of days wallowing in self-pity and then I shook it off. I was laboring against some residual health problems from my surgery, atrophy from my condition, and deep emotional wounds from my failing seven-year relationship. I jumped right into my thesis research and produced as many pages as I could. I sent Professor Caraja about a dozen pages by his May 21 deadline, but did not hear from him for weeks. Finally, on July 27 he sent me an edited version of the dozen pages that I had sent him for my thesis. In an attached letter he stated, "You are certainly on the right track and there are some

---

* Rob Capriccioso. "Hunter Settles Suicide Suit." *Inside Higher Ed.* https://www.insidehighered.com/news/2006/08/24/suicide. Accessed February 8, 2017.

good moments in the material you sent me. Of course, as you are well aware, you have a great deal of work to do." I knew how much toil lay ahead, but I was determined to finish.

I read through his comments and digested them, but did not have the luxury of applying the suggestions to my work because it was already early August and the retake of my exam was less than two months away. I knew I had to put the thesis aside and focus on preparing. Immediately I threw myself into the task of reviewing the information for my exam. This time the preparation was torture. I was burned out from my nearly constant work on the exam and thesis. It seemed that the harder I tried to absorb the information the less my brain wanted to retain it. I could not spend more than twenty minutes studying without all of my frustrations with Hunter swirling in my head and building to a crescendo that would force me to stop. In that period I felt lost and frustrated, and at times I just wanted to quit. But I told myself that I had worked hard to get to that point and if I could just sprint through the finish line and perform well on the test I would have only the thesis as the last hurdle before I would finally get my degree.

In order to take the exam again in the fall, I had to pay another fee to maintain my matriculation. After three years my time at Hunter started to feel like an unending cycle of fees, setbacks, and disappointments.

The following two journal entries demonstrate where my head was during my test preparation:

SEPTEMBER 19, 2011

I regret having gone to Hunter. My experience there has sapped my confidence in myself. I have been told over and over that nothing I do is good enough. It has turned what I thought would be one and a half to two years of hard work into three and a half years of academic work which has been clouded with ridiculous administrative trouble. Thinking about Hunter and what I've gone through there gives me nearly instant stress and anxiety, which I now have a hard time separating from the work that I am trying to complete. Rather than work hard and strive to do my best, I simply want to get it over with.

I have less respect for college educators because it seems that the department is full of sycophants who are more concerned with their own careers than the development of their students. There is an indifference to bringing along students like me who are passionate about the subject matter and teaching. It feels as if there is a disdain for any creative idea I have. The academics are secondary to the game of getting the degree itself and personal growth is hampered by inane obstacles rather than fostered by the institution.

I never thought that I would spend my days riddled with stress and anxiety while being frequently depressed. But I am usually exhausted and I still have many dark days. Often I just hope to get through the day. I put on a façade because I don't want to burden other people and have to admit to my weaknesses, sadness, etc. I am also increasingly filled with anger. I try to find positive outlets but my obsessive studying has put me into an intellectual prison. I have to meticulously remember specific argu-

ments of scholars and weigh them together in a historical context, and I feel that I am not absorbing anything. I am so burnt out, distraught, etc., that I can't study for more than fifteen minutes before my skin begins to tingle with frustration and I lose my focus. I'm tired of moving with fear of failure and the stress of trying to live up to other people's expectations. I'm ready to follow the path that my inner voice tells me to follow. I can envision a future far more beautiful than the present and I have to be strong enough to listen to my own voice and follow it.

SEPTEMBER 22, 2011

I have been spending as many hours as I can stomach without a meltdown, preparing for my comprehensive exam. Since I was only given about fifteen minutes to review the test I was only able to hurriedly jot down scant notes on what to improve upon. I have only three questions, yet I am still trying to master the central argument of two books on the first question and the test is one week away. It seems that nothing I do for this professor and Hunter College is ever good enough—there is always another hoop to jump through. His harsh words, chiding, and "high expectations" have completely psyched me out for the test. My brain feels like a sieve; nothing seems to be retained. I will continue to allocate as much time as I can to the test, but my feeling is that it won't be enough. As I try to study, the battles I have had with Hunter College over the past three-plus years keep playing in my head. It is hard to separate my poor experience there from the work I must perform at this point.

I flew into New York for the test and got a cheap hotel room in Jamaica, Queens. The hotel was the most cost-effective option and it made me realize why I hadn't spent much time in Jamaica. The hotel wasn't quite in the rough Southside Jamaica with which I had a fuzzy familiarity from 50 Cent's violent rap lyrics, but I could tell that I wasn't too far away. After checking in to my room, I set out to have dinner and treated myself to a small plate of paella and a glass of red wine at a Portuguese place up the street. I went back and reviewed my notes and then watched a little TV to relax. I turned off the TV at nine thirty and prepared to sleep. As I was drifting off I was jolted awake by screaming. I sat in my bed as a couple a few doors down had an intense, high-volume argument. The fight seemed to last forever. When things quieted down again, it was pushing eleven. The hair started to bristle on my neck because I was now awake and all of the same old torturous thoughts were running through my mind. I tried to sleep but people kept making noise in the hall. I started to think to myself, "Please, not again! Not another sleepless night before the test." This is what I wrote at the hotel on September 9, 2011, at 2 a.m.:

It's happening again. I can't sleep the night before my test. I have been popping one sleeping pill after another and nothing will allow me to fall asleep. The suicidal thoughts are creeping back into my head. The time at Hunter has ruined me as a person. I don't even believe in what I'm doing there anymore. I never wanted to go back to school. I am not living in line with my abilities. Academia is so absurd; this test is just a huge buildup for something of little importance. It will not define who I will be as a teacher or as a man. If anything, it has deterred me from wanting to con-

tinue an academic career and given me an inferiority complex. I feel worthless, angry, and flustered. I just want to walk away from it all and do my own thing but I don't want to quit when I am so close to finishing. But every time I feel close to finishing, a new unforeseen obstacle is thrown at me. I thought that this program would take no more than two years, at the absolute most. I have now been at Hunter for more than three years and I still have no guarantee that I will finish my degree. At this point I feel like I am forcing something that is unnatural and all of the pressure is devouring me. It doesn't make me want to do better work; it makes me want to give up or simply get it all over with. I am exhausted but I cannot sleep. When I try to rest, my mind comes alive with all my tribulations at Hunter and it makes me angry. I think of all the shit that I still have to do for this prick professor and it makes me want to walk into his office, spit in his face, and kick his ass, which wouldn't be difficult. I don't feel like I have anything to prove, but they are dangling this degree in front of me, which is nothing more than a credential to me at this point. I am too jaded and burned out to go after it. I do not like most of these professors; they are cold and I do not trust them. Mostly they are humorless, self-involved, and spiteful. The last thing I want is to become one of them. I can feel this system, experience, etc., changing me into a person that I don't like. I am bitter and misanthropic, and I feel like I have a shorter fuse. As a matter of fact, I think very little of myself in general and I am frequently uncomfortable in my own skin. Life feels like an endless chore and I have little desire to live long.

I woke up again after falling asleep about half an hour before my alarm went off. Bleary-eyed and exhausted, I forced myself to go down to the gym and exercise for twenty minutes to wake up. I went upstairs and took a cold shower afterward, and then took the train into Manhattan. I felt awful—very similar to how I'd felt before the first exam. When I reached Hunter I grabbed a large coffee and went into the test, ready to let it fly. I've never liked tests, but during my time at Hunter I had grown to hate them. Again, in a room full of people taking the comprehensive, I was the only one taking my particular exam. When my pen hit the paper the words flowed out. Surprisingly, I settled into a bit of a groove and everything felt a little better and more familiar than the first exam. When I finished I was sure I had finally passed, and I went out with my friends and celebrated.

For weeks I waited for the results, which I thought would only be a formality since I could not possibly have failed a second time after an improved performance. When I received the email from Professor Rosencrass informing me that I had once again failed my comp exam at Hunter, I flipped out. I am usually a fairly calm and even-tempered individual unless I am pushed to great lengths. I screamed nearly to the point of tears, swore, and threw things. In the email, Professor Rosencrass told me that he and the chair, Professor Belview, wanted to meet with me about my future in the program because, after two failed exams, I could be kicked out. The entire process had been psychologically damaging and draining in every way. I found out about the test because I checked my email as I was taking a break from working on my thesis, which was to be handed in to Professor Caraja at the end of January. But the retake of the test was at the end of February, so I would have to pay for the thesis and study again for the test, still with no guarantee of a degree. I was now three and a half years into the program, and the whole experience had made me question my desire to become a professor. I was uncertain that I would get a degree after investing even more exorbitant amounts of time and money.

I was amazed, because I worked much harder in a single year at Hunter than I ever did as an undergraduate, a fact that was reflected in my Hunter GPA of 3.6, compared to a 3.3 at Manhattanville. And at this stage in my life there were fewer distractions and I was completely engaged in the material. Rather than take the easy way out when studying, as I would have at Manhattanville so that I had more time for partying, I took the long road, trying to absorb as much information as possible. This time the interest was in the material itself, and I was driven to do additional reading and to seek out projects that were complex and difficult. I was drawn to them. Having had no previous experience studying Latin American history, due to the tragic death of the professor who held that position when I entered college as a freshman, I knew I was at a disadvantage. This profound discrepancy is a large part of why I worked so hard in and out of my classes at Hunter. I had learned most of what I knew from travel, independent reading, and having friends from Latin America. This meant that I had to do a great deal of side reading on many of the topics because much of the information was new to me or I had only had one sweep of it. I was learning as much as I could, as fast as possible.

Except for a couple of outstanding professors, the faculty I came in contact with at Hunter only talked about obstacles. The professors at Hunter who inspired me to learn and grow were rare exceptions. Generally, my professors at Hunter harped on the difficulty of getting jobs and similar topics that discouraged me to the point that I would continuously question myself as a student, as an aspiring teacher, and as a person. I entered Hunter because I wanted to be part of a noble profession that changed lives by encouraging young minds. My expressed desire to learn and teach was met with hollow protocol and tales of how their struggles were greater than mine. I found myself seriously considering leaving before the system changed me even further. During my long layoff, I considered all of these things and sent Professors Belview and Rosencrass a carefully worded letter about my situation (included in the appendix). After reading it, they told me to make an appointment to speak with both of them.

Chapter VI

Finally, I returned to Hunter in mid-November to see what they could do for me, after I had failed my exam for the second time. When I met with Belview and Rosencrass, they kept me waiting. In a microcosm of my experience with Hunter, I was ten minutes early and they were fifteen minutes late in getting the meeting started. I thought of a friend of mine who was beginning to enroll in the master's history program for education. He described Professor Rosencrass, whom he met with once for advice on classes, as a "dick." The best way I can describe most of the professors at the higher positions in the department is humorless, cold, inordinately self-important sycophants. As a result, I would feel that explaining my problems with fitting in with their system would be futile, if not detrimental. I tried to push this train of thought out of my mind as we began the meeting.

The three of us sat in Professor Belview's new office, which he was still in the process of moving into. It was the very same office where I had met with Professor Wallace for my first meeting at Hunter, when she assured me that it would be simple to gain entrance into the program if I was doing well in my classes. Professors Belview and Rosencrass were formal and courteous; they seemed somewhat sobered by the tone of my letter. They told me that they understood that I was a "good student" and, given my academic record, I should merit another attempt to pass the comprehensive exam, but they quickly emphasized the fact that they could, according to "Hunter policy," drop me from the program after two failed attempts. While my head was spinning from the fact that these men had just told me that they could send me home with nothing after I'd paid thousands of dollars and undergone years of toil, Professor Belview continued: "Unfortunately, Professor Caraja has decided that you are not up to his standards to work with, as he has concluded from your exam and the pages of thesis that you sent him. He says that his willingness to work on the thesis was contingent upon your performance on the exam; therefore, he will be unable to continue working with you."

I was shocked. I responded that, although Professor Caraja contended that his ability to work with me was contingent on my exams, it was not true; he had never mentioned this to me after he elected to take on my thesis. But I was quick to add that it did not matter since he was the unwilling party. As a result, they offered me a "deal": I had to find a new advisor to do an entirely different thesis with, and then I had to prepare to take the US history exam. If I agreed to this inane proposal, it would mean reading another forty to seventy new books for the exam, since these were the books that the US history majors would have read in their coursework. Then I would have to come up with a new thesis. It felt impossible for many reasons, but the fact that I had grown to distrust Hunter was perhaps the most burning.

When I explained to them that my confidence in the program and the people running it had been broken after I'd failed the exam, which was in Latino labor history, a subject that I was passionate about, they stared at me blankly. Now I was supposed to embark on another preparation for a US history exam? Then they reminded me, again, that I could have been thrown out of the program after two failed exams and they assured me that I was being given an opportunity, a second chance. I thought: how was I supposed to prepare for an exam in a history that was less important to me, and for which I hadn't studied at the graduate level? I told them that I had not been preparing for such an exam in my coursework, which meant starting the entirety of the list of US history books from scratch. I told them that it would make it very unlikely that I would be able to pass the first time, since I hadn't been able to pass an exam on a subject I had worked on for years.

Belview replied, "We think that you would probably pass on the first try. Most people do." This struck me as either a venal statement or an unrealistic one considering my history at Hunter, coming off of two failed exams. Then they returned to the topic of my thesis.

I told them that I was doing the thesis because I believed in it; because it was poignant and compelling. It was the type of history that I wanted to teach. I said that I would have gone to school for a MA in US history if that was what I'd wanted. They told me that if I was passionate about the subject and if my thesis project was as groundbreaking as I thought it would be, I could always write it as a book later in life—nothing was stopping me. But in order to get a degree I would have to find a workable thesis within the program, and the first step to doing that would be finding a new topic and a new advisor. I wanted to scream, because I had already spent hundreds of hours on my thesis and I felt it and everything else I had worked for slipping away. I felt powerless. But I calmed myself, knowing that I had no recourse, and that losing my cool would destroy everything I had invested in this degree. At the time, I had a feeling that this twisted token option with which they were presenting me was no better than having them tell me to go fuck myself. But I feared that my emotions were taking over and telling me this; it couldn't be the truth.

In the wake of the ravaging I had experienced at their hands, the entire chain of events that had led me to this moment flashed through my mind. Before I even entered the office, I knew that I had to hear what they had to say, smile, and shake their hands so I could have time to weigh the situation in my mind. I had to take time to find the best way to respond to their insulting offer. I left the office thirsty for relief and reprisal, totally unsure how I would lead the rest of my life.

When I made the decision to attend grad school, I did so out of a desire to make a living reading, writing, and teaching. I entered Hunter with high hopes, ready to focus on academics and a career. It had been nearly four years since I began this thirty-credit graduate program. If I'd had the desire, I could have become a lawyer with the time and effort I had spent. But I had altruistic and, I now admit, naïve intentions of being a teacher and making a difference in the classroom. Essentially, Hunter frustrated a well-intentioned student, who had done everything in his power to finish the degree, by making every step along the way absurdly difficult to the point of being destructive. I had applied to MA/PhD programs at several institutions, which advertise PhD degrees that take three to five years to complete in addition to the master's. Had I gotten into one of them, I would have probably completed a PhD in the time it would take me to get an MA at Hunter!

When I got home from NYC, I began to think. If I took their proposed course of study, I would have to return to Hunter to take a test on forty to seventy books that I had never read before. All the time, I would continue to pay to maintain matriculation in order to complete the requirements there and continue to incur more expenses for travel, lodging, food, and so on. This all would occur without a guarantee that I would receive a degree. The institution had failed to provide me with a tenable course of study for the three and a half years that I had been there and continuously pushed the degree further into my future. But they still couldn't promise me that I would receive my degree. Moreover, there is a time limit to how long someone can be in the program. Beyond four years after matriculating into the program one needs departmental permission for each subsequent semester. There were all sorts of ways they could take my time, efforts, and money and leave me with zilch. After several years, whenever I would think about Hunter College, I would get that awful feeling one gets when leaning over a cliff face staring down at death. Each time I had to go there to take a test or meet with professors, the feeling got worse. When I was there, everything was rushed and I constantly felt claustrophobic.

I spent the next several months pondering my situation. I didn't think it was right that I would be punished so severely for my failure on the exams. The capriciousness of Professor Caraja and the rigidity of Hunter had put me in an untenable position. I talked to every family member, friend, and educator I knew—nearly everyone with an opinion—and they all came to a similar conclusion: Hunter College was totally fucking me and I needed to do something drastic. In this society that meant one thing: lawyer up. I began my search of legal professionals locally and through contacts I had in New York City. After months of searching, I found the unfortunate answer. The kind of litigation I needed was sticky because big powerful schools (especially in the CUNY system) have legal teams and legal barriers to handle this sort of thing. No one would take it on without forcing me to pay a hefty retainer up front, and there was no guarantee that I would recoup any of my investment. The legal route was a dead end. I would most likely be throwing good money after bad.

I looked into transferring, but I would only be able to transfer a maximum of twelve credits of the twenty-seven I had earned, even if I transferred to another CUNY school. I would still have to do a thesis and perhaps another exam—not exactly a tantalizing option. I was running out of possibilities, so I felt that I only had one choice left: I began crafting a sober letter to the chancellor of Hunter. I decided that I would not just shrink away as they had probably expected; rather, I would tirelessly write letters until someone would help me. I'd write the chancellor of Hunter, the head of CUNY, and the New York State Board of Education if I needed to. I needed at least a modicum of satisfaction. Spring was passing into summer by the time I was putting my final touches on the carefully worded letter to the chancellor, when something truly remarkable happened.

Chapter VII

JUNE 3, 2012

Today I got an email from Professor Rosencrass telling me that they are changing the program and they will no longer be requiring a comprehensive exam in order to receive a degree. After I had failed twice they were doing away with the requirement. I was shocked. He advised me to find a primary and secondary reader for a new thesis, and I had a breakdown. Normally one would be thrilled with such news, but given my history with Hunter it felt like a cold stab at reconciliation from an ex-lover that one had grown to despise. But given my desperate situation, if I still entertained the idea of teaching at the college level, I would have to forge on. Part of me wondered if this was not some evil trick (when dealing with Hunter College one can never be too sure). However, if only a thesis is standing between me and the possibility of teaching at the college level the proposition was at least mildly interesting. But how can I trust these shysters? How can I go crawling back?

Then there is the prospect that they will not allow me to do the thesis I am working on because there is no primary reader, except Caraja, at the institution.

I knew that there was nothing that I could do to benefit my situation during the summer months when the professors were on vacation and I was working at the height of the busy season as a bartender. It was hard enough to get anything done during the semester. I agonized over the decision for weeks. If I returned to write the thesis, I would still have to find an advisor and secondary reader from the full-time faculty, and most of the faculty who were still employed there, with whom I had a rapport, were adjuncts. However, I knew I could not go to the chancellor in light of this new development because it would jeopardize the opportunity.

After an agonizing period of research and weighing my options, I decided that I would return and write a new thesis, knowing that it was the only foreseeable obstacle standing between me and the elusive degree. I wrote Professor Rosencrass, telling him that I was interested in taking their offer to write a new thesis with a different advisor. I scheduled an appointment to meet with him at Hunter as soon as the semester commenced.

I began doing side reading and considering the faculty who could advise a potential thesis. I realized that there were only four possible candidates: Professor Angelico, the undergraduate advisor from whom I had taken Historical Methods. Professor Stein, a helpful, soft-spoken grandfatherly figure who taught my Intellectual History class. Professor Regresso, who I thought would be an excellent candidate to oversee a thesis related to Latin American history. If all else failed, there was Professor Rosencrass. He could be approached because I had a relationship with him and was once again placing my future in his hands. However, any topic that related to my degree program would be well outside of his area of expertise.

I wrote Professor Regresso first, because I thought she was the leading candidate. I sent her the email below in late July of 2012.

Dear Professor Regresso,

I hope you are doing well. I thoroughly enjoyed your class, Colonial Latin American History, which I found challenging and informative, as well as fun. I thought your one-page recaps of the reading that you had us perform was a good way to get me to reassess the reading and think critically about what I had read, which is a technique I hope to employ when I teach.

I am writing you because I am trying to find an adviser for a potential thesis and Professor Rosencrass recommended I speak with you. I was previously working with Professor Caraja, but I was unable to develop a rapport with him because we never had a class together. Since I took Colonial Latin America from you, I have been desperately trying to complete my degree; however, due to a number of difficult occurrences outside of my control, I have been unable to finish. I would be happy to provide you with the details of my travails, but I will not bore you with them now. I believe that we worked well together and now, without the fetter of a comprehensive exam, I would be grateful for an opportunity to work with you on my thesis and to complete my degree. I understand, as we had spoken before, that the thesis that I worked on with Professor Caraja on Latino labor in western New York is outside your area of expertise, however, I am most willing to abandon the project and focus on something that is more centered on Latin America.

While working on my final paper in Modern Mexico, I became interested in the history of the U.S. drug wars in Mexico. As I was researching for the paper, I did a great deal of reading about the greater U.S. drug war in Latin America. I would be interested in focusing on the general history or some aspect of the history of the U.S. drug wars in

Latin America which I would hope you could guide me into a feasible project combining your knowledge and strengths with my desire to learn to make the best project possible. However, I am very flexible and I am willing to work together to find a suitable project which falls under the purview of your specific academic knowledge. If it would be at all possible to work together, I would appreciate your finding a convenient time for us to meet and discuss a project at the beginning of the fall semester. Thank you very much for your time and consistent aid in my academic pursuits.

Best,
Loren Mayshark

She swiftly sent me a curt response via BlackBerry that stressed the importance of her work and essentially chided me for asking her to advise my thesis. She said that I should speak to someone in the US history department since I didn't have the background to attempt anything relating to Latin American history. She closed this response by saying "Best of luck."

I was initially discouraged that my first option had brushed me off so swiftly, and I had a nagging feeling that she didn't want to understand my situation. I imagined that to her this multi-year odyssey I had been on was an annoying trifle. Although I was a little disheartened, I had made up my mind that I would not be thwarted. I forwarded the email to Professor Rosencrass, along with my concerns, and he sent me a clipped response via BlackBerry in which he said he imagined I was disappointed and that we should "adjust the focus" of my thesis in order to complete the degree. He suggested that I spend the rest of the summer thinking of who I would like to advise the thesis and then shape that to the expertise of the professor.

I knew that I had to be careful as to how I would prepare for meeting with potential thesis advisors in the fall, especially since I had the unsettling feeling that Professor Regresso either did not grasp or did not care to grasp what I was proposing. After losing my finest candidate without a face-to-face meeting, I knew I could not afford to burn through the rest of the candidates via email. I needed a carefully designed plan tailored to each of the remaining professors so that I could get one of them to advise my thesis.

Here was my plan: I would bone up on my intellectual history and come up with a couple of potential topics that I could work on with Professor Stein. Also, I would look into Professor Angelico's area of expertise and see if there were any parallels between my thesis on Latino labor and his area of interest, which mostly dealt with colonial US history and nineteenth-century US history. I would also continue to research US drug policy in Latin America with the hopes that, as a last-ditch effort, I could get Professor Rosencrass to jointly advise that thesis with the aid of the kind and brilliant Professor Rodriguez at Lehman College. I pored over thousands of pages of diverse historical materials in the weeks leading up to my meetings at Hunter, which were scheduled for the beginning of fall semester, 2012.

When I left for New York City, I had set up meetings with Professors Angelico and Rosencrass. I could not get hold of Professor Rodriguez or Professor Stein; I would have to do my best to seek them out when I got to New York. When I arrived at 68th Street and Lexington Avenue on Tuesday, August 28, I went up to the fifteenth floor of the Hunter West building, to the history department, and met with Professor Rosencrass. I found out that I was unable to get hold of Professor Stein because he was on sabbatical that semester, a surprising revelation that immediately eliminated him as a potential advisor. I told Professor Rosencrass that I had a meeting with Professor Angelico later in the week and if he was unable or unwilling to advise my thesis then I was out of options. It was at this time that I suggested that he advise my thesis, since he was the only remaining full-time faculty member that I had any relationship with. He seemed surprised at first, and then I explained that Professor Rodriguez had mentioned that he would consider working with me on a potential project. He sat back in his chair looking pensive, and then said, "First talk to Professor Angelico, and if he will not undertake the project, then I will consider making an exception . . ." He trailed off and I eagerly awaited the rest of his response. "I will consider being the de jure first reader," he continued, "if this professor . . . what is his name?"

"Rodriguez," I replied.

"Yes, Rodriguez. If he would consider being the de facto primary reader, we could possibly work something out."

I thanked him and vowed to spend the next few days vigorously pursuing a tenable thesis plan, but I knew I had my work cut out for me. These professors had no problem blowing me off, and I was rapidly running out of options.

When I left Hunter, I hopped on the six train and went to Harlem, where I transferred to the four train, which took me to the Bronx. As I got on the four, I thought about all of the times I had crammed onto that train in Harlem, taking the ride to the Lehman College subway stop, worrying that I would miss even a few moments of Professor Rodriguez's engaging classes. Back when I was taking courses, it felt imperative to attend every class possible. Now I was going up to the

Bronx to save my degree. When I reached the history department, I found out that Professor Rodriguez had office hours on Wednesday. I noted the hours; I would return the next day.

I was sleeping on a friend's couch in Brooklyn and the trip to Lehman, door to door, was close to two hours. When I returned the next day I was nervous. I knew in my bones that if this man either was not there or did not want to help me, the opportunity to do an interesting thesis related to my area of study would vanish. When I got to his office, at the very beginning of his office hours, the door was closed. I stood outside expecting the worst. "He's not here," I thought. I took a deep breath, and then knocked. After what seemed like several minutes the door opened slowly. Standing behind the door was Professor Rodriguez, his wise face sporting a small gray beard that parted into a smile as soon as he recognized me. He invited me in and instructed me to sit. As I launched into describing the situation, he listened carefully, something that people rarely seemed to do anymore, especially most of the professors I had had. It is as if they are so used to lecturing in class that they continue to lecture outside of the classroom, comfortable hearing their own voices. After listening, he said that he would be happy to help. He understood that I had had a difficult time working on my degree and he said that he knew I was a serious student and that I should be allowed to graduate after investing so much time, money, and hard work. He told me to keep him posted and he would do the best he could to accommodate my situation. It was a refreshingly simple and human interaction, something incredibly rare in my experience at Hunter College. I thanked him profusely and left feeling better than I had in a long time.

The following day I met with Professor Angelico. When I stepped into his office, he wore a smile and was extremely friendly. He was a jovial, gregarious, razor-sharp Greek-American who had studied at Hunter himself. I explained my situation and he was sympathetic. However, he said that his area of expertise was very far from anything that I could integrate into my field of study. He contended that I would be better off finding someone who worked more closely in my area of interest. He did add that he would be willing to work on something if I had absolutely no other option, but he truly believed that for my sake I should seek someone else. I thanked him for his candor and kindness, and left with a cloudy feeling of uncertainty.

I returned to my friend's apartment in Brooklyn. It was my second-to-last night in New York. I had a meeting the following morning with Professor Rosencrass that would determine my fate at Hunter College. I was tired and stressed out. My friend suggested we relax and get dinner and a couple of drinks. That sounded perfect. We met up with some fun friends from undergrad. The night of sharing tales and laughter was refreshingly soothing, but I lost track of time and drinks. I did not return to sleep on his couch until well after midnight. When I awoke the next morning, I had a hangover and was painfully unrested after squirming around for hours, trying to get comfortable on his couch. I was already running late for my appointment. My buddy gave me a bottle of water and I dashed to the train. The hour-plus ride to Hunter was torturous. I was nervous and felt that I had really fucked up. It was that kind of creeping guilt one gets after a night of revelry, but this was worse. I was not staying as focused as I should and was jeopardizing my future.

When I got to Hunter, I picked up an apple and banana from the kind man at the fruit stand out front. I forced down both pieces of fruit, but still felt uneasy. I thought that a cup of coffee would straighten me out and sharpen me up for the meeting. As I mentioned earlier, I am extremely sensitive to caffeine so I generally only consume coffee in a pinch. I got a large cup of joe with cream and hustled up to Rosencrass's office. When I arrived he was with a student and there was another grad student waiting to meet with him. I collapsed on the floor outside his office and quenched my thirst with the hot coffee. My heart beat wildly and the stress was cutting into my stomach like a sharp blade. I started to feel woozy. The fellow graduate student waiting outside Rosencrass's office happened to be one I had taken a class with in my final semester. I was shocked that he was still in the program. He recognized me and struck up a conversation. I did my best to listen and act normal while adjusting to all of the changes going on in my body, anxiety mixing with guilt and caffeine. I mostly listened and gave the occasional nod or one-word remark as he told me about the particularities of his travails at Hunter. His story was not as absurd as mine, but it seemed that Hunter was not making it easy on him either.

He droned on, and in the midst of the conversation I began to feel legitimately sick and the hallway began swimming. While he was in midsentence, I abruptly stood up, muttered "Excuse me," and walked hurriedly down the hall. As I got to the door that said "History" on it, the department headquarters, I felt that awful telltale tingling under my tongue that told me that I was going to vomit. It felt like the harbinger of death. I broke into a sprint, hoping I could make it down one flight of stairs to the men's room. I couldn't. I started to puke in my mouth as I ran to a garbage can with flaps on either side. I pushed one of the flaps back and stuck my head inside the can so I could vomit a long, painful spew. When I pulled my head out of the trash, I looked around, half-expecting the entire history department to be standing there laughing or staring at me in disbelief and admonishment. Thankfully, the coast was clear. I immediately headed down one flight of stairs to the men's room. I washed my hands and face. Then I looked into the mirror, feeling like a ghost. This was my strange reality. What was I doing? What had I become?

When I returned to Professor Rosencrass's office, the student ahead of me was just finishing with him. I felt better, but still in disarray. As the student exited, Professor Rosencrass saw me waiting and called me into his office. When our eyes met he asked how I was doing. I forced a smile and told him, "Great!" He returned the forced pleasantries and both of us seemed relieved after he asked me to take a seat. He launched into the discussion about my thesis, inquiring if I had found a primary reader. I explained what Professor Rodriguez had offered me in the chance meeting we'd had on Wednesday. After I spoke, he sat back in his chair, folding his hands together as he pondered the situation. My stomach was churning as I sat across from him. I was nervous and my equilibrium was off. I hoped I wouldn't vomit on his desk. I thought in that moment, as I sat listening to him drone on, how marvelous I felt compared to how I had felt a few moments before, when I had that nasty run-in with the garbage can. He leaned toward me and said, "This is what I am willing to do: I will act as the de jure primary reader and he will act as the de facto. You can submit the thesis to me, chapter by chapter, and I will look at aspects such as scholarship, writing proficiency, grammar, et cetera. He will make sure that the information is correct, and he will oversee the actual content of the thesis..."

As he droned on, I thought: Rosencrass is giving me an opportunity. I could conceivably finish the degree! I discussed some of the particulars of how I would proceed, and thanked him profusely for the opportunity. As I left his office I felt elated, as if I had stolen a victory from the clutches of an almost certain defeat. I had defied all odds and was back in the hunt.

I spent the next couple of months furiously reading up on the subject of US drug policy in Latin America. I purchased dozens of books related to the topic. I tailored my work schedule to prepare for a move to New York, maximizing the amount of time I spent working on my thesis. I arranged everything in my life so that I could stay in New York. I was planning on subletting a place for a couple of months so that I could reap the maximum benefit from the time and so that I could work closely with my professors, perhaps speeding up the process. I started to believe that I could complete the program in time to gain valuable experience and perhaps some much-needed monetary compensation by working as an adjunct professor the following fall, as I had promising leads on a couple of positions at local colleges.

Chapter VIII

On Friday, October 19, 2012, I arrived with my father and wonderful cousin Finn in the greater NYC area. We stayed in a budget hotel in New Jersey, taking daily trips into the city to visit with friends and family. We had a blast. Then on Sunday, Superstorm Sandy hit. I said my good-byes to my father and cousin as they hightailed it out of the city before the storm. I was stuck in the city, drinking beer at a pricey Mexican bar and restaurant near Grand Central, contemplating my options. My mother called, urging me to leave. I finished my beer and snapped into action.

I got on the last train for Connecticut, where I decided I would wait out the storm at my good friend Rue's house. When I boarded the train I was astonished to see how packed it was. Every seat was taken, and I thought they must have oversold the train. As I surveyed the faces of my fellow passengers, there seemed to be a mix of consternation and exhaustion. After a memorably tense ride, I arrived at my friend's house as the storm was starting to set in.

We lost power for thirty-six hours, and trees were down, but compared to the tragic stories in the news about the many victims of the powerful storm, we escaped relatively unscathed. I was in no position to return to New York in the wake of Sandy, so my friend selflessly offered to let me stay with him indefinitely. I set up my laptop and furiously went to work on my thesis.

In a few weeks, I produced a full proposal, including an outline and preliminary bibliography, which I submitted to both professors. Then I went to work on a sample chapter at the behest of Professor Rosencrass. The sample chapter was to be the first chapter of the thesis after the introduction. Each professor had his own philosophy about how I should proceed. Professor Rodriguez suggested that after submitting the sample chapter I should continue to write the thesis straight through to the end so I could have a better sense of where I was going with the project. This approach made sense to me. However, Professor Rosencrass said that the proper way to proceed would be chapter by chapter, not moving forward until he deemed each chapter in top shape. Since he was the primary reader and my future at Hunter rested in his hands, his approach would prevail.

When I first started work on the thesis, it was with great enthusiasm because (although I still believed that I'd been greatly wronged and it was the least they could do) I felt that I was being given an opportunity to finish my degree. Although it wasn't as exciting or groundbreaking as my initial thesis, in which I had invested hundreds if not thousands of hours, it was still something I had a profound interest in. I was excited to get back to work, and I eagerly pored over the information. As I worked on the thesis, I felt I was making progress, working closely with my professors while having the vast resources of the Hunter Library and CUNY system at my disposal. I worked tirelessly to produce the preliminary bibliography (approximately fifty books and articles), outline, and sample chapters.

I did not fully understand that this arrangement was doomed from the outset. I moved home after a couple of months of intense effort. Then, six months later, while rewriting chapter after chapter to Professor Rosencrass's dissatisfaction, I hired a professional editor to help me with my thesis. She had worked with several published authors. Professor Rosencrass had changed the agreed-upon outline in the midst of my efforts to complete the thesis. The editor was helping me organize my thoughts and adjust to the new outline. After reading drafts for one year, she said, "I have no idea what will please this man," and quit. I was discouraged, but I pressed on. The following journal entries capture how I felt when I was deeply immersed in the thesis process.

JUNE 12, 2013

Ever since I enrolled at Hunter, the school has been a weight on me that has narrowed my options and sapped my strength. I have been in this thirty-credit program for five years now, and for most of the time it has been the major focus of my life. Hunter has been so consuming that I have had little time for other endeavors, and I have only been able to earn just enough to sustain myself. I can't plan for the future because I have never known when this was going to end and I haven't been able to walk away because throughout the entire process they have strung me along, making it seem that graduation is imminent. Now it seems interminable, and although Professor Rosencrass has claimed that finishing my thesis will offer a tenable path to graduation, my fundamental trust in the institution has been broken. So I live in constant uncertainty about whether or not my efforts will lead to completion of the degree that I initially set out after, which I have now more than paid for financially and with my efforts and time commitment. This process has worn away my psyche and my resolve, and has turned me from a person skeptical of the academic setting to someone who feels academia is something I don't want to continue in now, perhaps ever. Oddly, I still have a desire to teach and I don't know if or how I ever will. I originally attended Hunter because I truly believed that I could make a difference as an educator at the college level, and I was passionate about my subject. But after the mental drubbing I continue to endure from my professors and the institution I feel lost, apathetic, and at times acutely angry.

I am now rewriting my first chapter for the sixth time. I have produced nearly one hundred pages of draft but Prof. Rosencrass insists that I return to the starting line again each time. I have appreciation for the thesis process and making students earn their degrees by exhorting them to do their best work. But this is the second thesis I have been working on and the previous tests I took, which cost me countless hours and hundreds of dollars in expenses, amounted to absolutely nothing. This personal history, coupled with the uncertainty I still feel in not knowing if I will do enough to finish this thesis to finally graduate in December, makes it extremely difficult to focus on it and stay the course. I feel that my trust has been broken again and again, so it is hard to muster the energy and focus this late in the game, one year after I started this thesis and five years after I started this degree, while I've faced nothing but obstacles—artificial bureaucratic and pedagogic mush that has gotten in the way of my education.

I have committed and exerted myself now as I have in no other endeavor in my academic career and perhaps in the entirety of the rest of my life. All I see is disorganization and barriers; it seems that the onus is always put on me when there is a task. I no longer see hope in my situation. The thesis and graduate school put me in an intellectual prison where I don't have time to pursue all of the other exciting interests.

I can see why many academics get caught in the narrow focus of their discipline or sub-discipline, because the competitive nature of academia means that one could spend a lifetime acquiring credentials while delving deeper into a topic, reading, writing, lecturing, attending conferences, consulting, etc., without ever doing any meaningful inquiry outside of their discipline. I feel pigeonholed in my particular field, and I also don't have the confidence that I know enough to teach it. Nor have I been prepared to stand in front of a classroom and teach in my five years at Hunter.

Although I started this current thesis with the fire of inspiration and exuberance, now, on my sixth draft, all the blood has been drained from the project and I am simply left with a feeling of drudgery. This project and program have done the opposite of what I would hope for my students. Rather than serve as an inspiration for them to gain deeper knowledge of the subject and feed a hunger to learn, this has made me question academia, exhausted me on the subject, and put me in a situation where I am strongly revaluating my life.

SEPTEMBER 20, 2013 (This is a journal entry about a meeting that occurred around September 14.)

I had a meeting with Professor Rosencrass, and the first thing he told me was that it would be impossible to finish the degree by spring, which made me feel immediately dejected. He told me that I was not creating the proper historical context, and when I asked him how to do so he told me that he could not show me. He simply said, "You just know it when you see it." Later I asked him about his problem with my transitions and how they could be better utilized to build historical context, and he told me, "I can't give you a formula; you must look at the historians you admire and try to understand how they are accomplishing the feat of writing compelling history." This confused me. "Shouldn't he be able to actually teach me?" I wondered.

When we met he went through my paper fairly thoroughly. At times the comments felt so cutting that I started to feel angry, as if I was being mentally bludgeoned, but I said nothing and continued to nod and listen. It often felt that speaking honestly about my frustration was futile, because he would constantly interrupt me and tell me how it was more difficult for him or how it takes time to do something really well. Often I have felt that he and other professors are quick to criticize, slow to praise, and frequently speak over me, asserting their points until mine are drowned out.

As the meeting started to wind down I pulled out the Degree Audit Application Form (DAAF) that I needed to graduate and tried to ask him some questions about it. He quickly told me that it was very unlikely that I would be able to finish by December and that it was too early to discuss this sort of thing. Immediately, anger welled up in me. When I started to express disappointment he asked what the hurry was and I told him that I had possible academic work. He seemed surprised that I was in a hurry to finish so I could teach. I told him that if I was able to finish my degree I had some promising leads on adjunct work in my area. I had a better future in sight, which I had worked hard for. He said that I could only do the thesis once and so to "get it right" I had to work as hard as possible under his tutelage as he sat there and tore through the sixth version of my first chapter. My hair was bristling with frustration. He paused and gazed off into the city in the distance as he told me that all the institutions I sought employment with would be looking at this project as they made their decisions.

I thought to myself that I had felt much more confident about a year ago when I was doing some guest lecturing at the college level, and this process was sapping my confidence and hope. As this has dragged on it feels interminable and with the finish line constantly pulled away from me it gets increasingly exhausting and arduous, and the blood is drained from the piece. The defeats are having a negative cumulative impact that makes each step I take increasingly uncomfortable, I thought as I sat there. Seeing the pained expression on my face, he softened his tone a little, and he said that he knew that I could do better work if I only would take the time to produce the best possible example of my work, "because all these schools will be looking at this." I inhaled deeply and all I could do was nod. He continued, "You only get to do this once," and my dejection inhibited me, at the time, from seeing the irony in his words, this being my second attempt at a thesis.

I notice that Professor Rosencrass is quick to criticize, but he is never able to explain how to correct the error; he almost never praises. For example, on the sixth draft of my first chapter he twice wrote, "This is not an effective conclusion," but he failed to tell me why or tell me how to write an effective one. He simply stated, "How about summary?" When I asked him specific questions about how to improve he said that one simply knows what good historical writing is when one sees it. He advised me to see how historians I admire do it and try to learn from or, I guess, emulate their style. This gives me the nagging feeling that I am just ambling about in the dark, trying to please this man, but I don't know exactly what to do to be effective. I just come to know the many aspects of my work that do not please him. I have lost so much confidence that I feel I am losing my ability to read critically, think imaginatively, and write clearly.

Every time I have to resubmit a chapter it derails my progress. It is extremely difficult to motivate myself with anything besides simply getting it done. The entire process has taken such a psychological toll. Having multiple professors deride my work and having one drop me has sapped my confidence. Professor Rosencrass has balked every time I have mentioned teaching, insisting that no one should teach at the college level without a PhD. Also I feel that I was not well versed in any particular area of study because I have had to cobble my degree together from the seven or so graduate classes offered every semester and perhaps only one per semester is relevant to Latin American history.

NOVEMBER 11, 2013

Rosencrass wrote on my paper that the source base on my seventh draft was "incredibly thin." Obviously I wasn't going to break my neck to source this document for the seventh time as I have been changing and cutting large pieces throughout the project. It is exhausting to the point of it being extremely taxing and I have started to have fantasies about walking into his office and beating the shit out of him and then going to the hallway and confronting other faculty members. But I know that it has just become a long grind and if I can continue to endure the psychological pain, I hope that I will be able to complete the degree. But the process has become nearly joyless, with the exception of the moments when I still fall into the trance of the reading, especially from some fresh, adroit prose in the genre, or when I actually still get a little joy from turning a phrase myself or catch the rare flow in my thesis writing. The process has sapped my confidence in myself as a writer, thinker, historian, and man. I feel that my brain is a sieve and I don't retain anything. I am starting to wonder if I will ever possess the ability or right to speak with any authority on any subject.

Teaching seemed like an attractive option and meaningful route. At times it still does, but this experience has given me a visceral revulsion for academia and the feeling that I am horribly unprepared to teach anything. I don't know if I'll ever recover. Looking back on my time, the majority of my feedback has been negative and positive feedback has largely come from a precious few talented, thoughtful professors that I've had. I know that I must be a mature student, open to criticism, if I am perform-

ing well at the graduate level, but there have been no memorable instances of positive reinforcement of my draft from Prof. Rosencrass. I have begun to deeply question my intellect and abilities, especially with the backdrop of multiple failures in my writing and my personal life. The thesis project has filled me with a feeling of incompetence. Rather than nurture my ability to learn, prepare me to teach, or encourage me to feel that I would be a good educator with faith in our education system, it has done the opposite.

DECEMBER 16, 2013

I just received comments back on my latest chapter from a friend of the family who has been helping me with this process since my editor quit. The man has multiple English degrees and a PhD in education, and said that my work seems solid, coherent, and every bit what Professor Rosencrass had requested. Judging from the various pertinent documents and the seventh version of chapter one, which he was kind enough to edit for me before I send it in to Rosencrass, he said that I seemed to be on track. He thinks that Rosencrass's demands are excessive and he must be "on some ego trip and seems to be taking it out on you." The other professional editor who had been working with me found it impossible to believe his demands and she eventually quit. In my seventh draft I have produced the most dryly academic draft yet.

JANUARY 11, 2014

I submitted my seventh draft to him on 12/18 and he replied that he would look at it in the next couple of weeks. It is now 1/11/14 and I have *yet to hear from him. This wouldn't be a big deal if it were not for the history that I have had with Hunter and Prof. Rosencrass. I have been at this for approximately six years now and I have been working on the thesis as the central focus of my life for a year and a half. I am exhausted, and I will spend another semester bartending and covering some of my friend's classes at SUNY Fredonia, for free, to gain more experience.*

At this point I feel so burned out by the entire experience that I simply want to finish. Six years in and I am still at the mercy of this man and this institution, with no guarantee of finishing. I have signed another $180 check to the school to maintain matriculation.

The expense of the thesis is not simply the money paid to Hunter College. It is the up-front costs plus the number of penalty fees because their rigid policies and bureaucratic ineptitude made it nearly impossible to pay. Also, there is rent in New York, transportation, etc.; I am still paying to go to New York City for thesis-related minutiae. Additionally, there is the cost of books bought for the classes, the theses, side reading, etc. I have found that in the course of writing my thesis I have incurred a great amount of unforeseen expenses. I think of the hundreds or thousands of dollars spent on food, supplies in the Hunter bookstore, coffees, etc. The tens of thousands of dollars spent, the debt incurred, the mental pain, the frustration, the stress, the lost wages in cutting back on my hours at the many part-time jobs I have worked to support myself the best I can during this marathon run at an MA in history is maddening.

There continue to be logistical costs, book costs, paper costs, etc. My personal debt since enrolling in the program (which was advertised at a cost of about $10,000) is over $16,000, and the amount of money spent, considering how I have altered my life, is more than $30,000. All the while I have not been able to settle into a permanent position because of the time and effort grad school has taken: the mental toll, lack of time, etc. Constantly thinking that I am about to finish while having the finish line cruelly moved further from me has worn me down. The life I have been forced to live because of my academic pursuit has been causing me to fall back on bartending or other impermanent part-time work.

MARCH 7, 2014

I just finished a phone conversation with Professor Rosencrass. I had specific questions about my work but he simply dominated the entire session, zealously telling me about all the faults in my work. It was hard to get a word in edgewise. Every time I asked him how I could better prepare something he would simply say, "I can't tell you how to do this. You should be getting a sense from reading all of these history books as to how it is done well by professional historians." Everything is swimming in my head; nothing makes sense anymore. I don't know up from down in this process. What I have been asked to do has changed so many times that I am simply trying to please my advisor so I can move on in the process. It is a quagmire that I cannot help getting depressed about. Every time I try to express my opinion or ask about something he seems to get irritated. It seems that he isn't teaching me anything, just constantly pointing out my mistakes and telling me that I need to fix them.

March 8, 2014

I feel helpless and trapped, with a growing sense of inadequacy. I will never be great at anything. I still have suicidal thoughts, but I don't have the strong desire to do it. Sometimes I hope that death will just come. I find myself doing self-destructive things and sometimes that is enough to take the edge off of the pain I feel. I never thought that attending Hunter would turn into this kind of painful rage, but it has combined with other factors into an inescapable malaise. I never thought it would drag on so long. So far I have produced nothing that seems to have value in my thesis.

By hijacking the entire process yesterday, Rosencrass made it impossible to ask the questions I wanted to ask and it has made the process much longer than I thought it would be. He has not, as far as I remember, put one positive comment on my paper. At this level I know that I am not looking to be showered with compliments. However, it seems that every single interaction I have with him is negative and there is no positive reinforcement. It seems that he can only point out what is wrong with my work, only break me down as a student. But there is no actual teaching. He is not saying that certain points or techniques are good and telling me how to use them in building something better, thus helping me grow as a student. He is being purposely harsh and difficult. His controlling style, in which he talks over me and insists upon dominating the discussion of my paper, inhibits my ability to have a two-sided discussion and receive answers to the questions I have about my paper.

MARCH 13, 2014

Professor Rosencrass and I had a phone meeting set for 2:15. He didn't call until 2:48 and apologized by saying that he was in a meeting with the president of Hunter. I told him that I understood and then he told me that he had very little time to go over the material. We had a hurried discussion and he said he had to go by 3 p.m. Terribly little was accomplished. I am left feeling cheated and confused. Every meeting with my professors is rushed and I never feel that I am getting the information necessary to advance my work in the way they envision it.

MARCH 14, 2014

Professor Caraja and Professor Rosencrass are both grossly hung up on the minutest details of my writing. Both have cited my paragraphs as a problem in my construction. When speaking of my paragraphs in reference to my first failed exam, Caraja said that two-sentence paragraphs were unacceptable at the graduate level. But in the test there was no time to reread it, much less alter something like paragraph structure, which is impossible to fix without a fresh bottle of whiteout. I had no time to revise. Professor Rosencrass also has been adamant about my paragraphs rigidly following a topic sentence with a single thought. I was excoriated by both professors on many aspects of my writing; interestingly, they both came down hard on my paragraphing. This got me thinking.

Paragraphs are more of a subjective aspect of writing than many others. In fact, there have been several studies that show paragraphing is not a standard objective aspect of writing, and even topic sentences can be handled differently by different writers. Arthur A. Stern conducted a paragraphing experiment where they had one hundred English teachers divide a five-hundred-word chunk of text from Cleanth Brooks and Robert Penn Warren's Fundamentals of Good Writing *into paragraphs. The results varied significantly, with only five participants dividing the piece as Warren and Brooks had. This led Stern to wonder: "If, as the handbooks declare, a paragraph represents a 'distinct unit of thought,' why is it that we can't recognize a unit of thought when we see one? If every paragraph contains an identifiable topic sentence, then why don't all of us identify the same topic sentence?"* Although the paragraph is a subjective unit, their versions of it were presented to me as fact and I was treated like a clod who simply could not grasp the proper technique. Ultimately, this contributed to my failure on my comprehensive exams and evidence that I was an inferior student by Professor Caraja. It was also one of the shortcomings in my prose that inhibited me from producing an acceptable first chapter.*

Many professors, but not all, carry themselves seriously and seem to have some hidden agenda that exists in their mind, and any way that I present the material that does not meet that expectation is unacceptable. After being bludgeoned thoroughly by Professor Caraja and continuously assailed by Professor Rosencrass, I am mentally exhausted. It is to the point that I have lost my focus, drive, and passion, and now I am simply gutting this process out in a joyless slog. Therefore, I don't know how to write, I am no longer concerned with the craft of writing history, the artistry; I'm simply trying to get it done, coldly, so I can gain a piece of paper so I can be paid to teach. Now I don't work hard to artfully craft an en-

---

* Arthur A. Stern. "When Is a Paragraph?" College Composition and Communication 27, no. 3 (1976): 253–57. doi:10.2307/357044.

gaging and well-put-together paper. I am reactive. I'm trying to guess at what he wants, please his predilections, for the lone purpose of finally ending this torment.

APRIL 2, 2014

Today I met with the history department secretary, Joseph Stone, a kind, balding man with thick glasses and the look of a career librarian, to talk about the steps I must take to finish my thesis. When I asked him how he was doing, he replied that he was exhausted and felt a little worn down. He mentioned that most professors would go on break while he would remain at Hunter during the summer. I told him that Hunter should give him a well-deserved tropical vacation and he replied that he had gone on a cruise three weeks ago, but "This place has a way of draining people . . . now it almost feels as if I have never left." I smiled and told him that I had an understanding of where he was coming from and that I don't get why everyone is so serious, and he replied, "It is as if they want everyone to be miserable here." When I discussed my path toward graduation with him he told me that it seemed as if I was on the right track and that he appreciated how proactive I had been in making sure I had handled every administrative aspect of my degree. I replied that I have learned through past administrative difficulties that I must do everything I can, dot every i and cross every t, or else I would be in a world of trouble. I told him that I was willing to do whatever it took to finish. After we met I went back to the Hunter library and continued working on journal articles for the NYU conference in the field that I was in town for.

I took a break from reading journal articles for the conference to recharge with a cup of coffee. Hunter has subcontracted most of its coffee operation out to Starbucks. I rarely drink coffee, but decided to go all out and enjoy a white chocolate mocha with whipped cream (if you're going to go, go all the way!). When I ordered it I requested the lid on the side because I didn't want the steam to melt my whipped cream—a standard practice of mine on the rare occasions when I indulge. What happened next is indicative of how Hunter operates: the woman pouring the coffee told me that she had to put the lid on because "that's the rules." When I began to explain my request for the lid on the side, ensuring her that I would put it on at the appropriate time, she cut in as I was still finishing my sentence and said, "If someone gets burned, then I'm liable." I bit my lip, not wanting to escalate the situation, and then told her that putting a lid on was fine.

Nearly every employee, from advisors, administrators, professors, right down to the people who brew the coffee at Hunter, is reactive, often rude, and indignant to basic requests if one deviates at all from what their interpretation of Hunter policy is. Most are inordinately nervous that their conduct will reflect poorly on themselves if they do anything that does not rigidly fit into their job description. This cup of coffee is but one example of how seemingly normal people almost instantly devolve into angry beasts when I make the simplest inquiries or requests. It was maddening when I was a student in the program here, but now that I have finished the coursework and my visits to Hunter have become less frequent, I have enough separation to occasionally laugh at the insanity of it all. As a re-

sult of my distance I can see better the inefficiency and inhumanity that make this place a raincloud. It still amazes me, however, that an educational institution, which is run like a business, can have such poor customer service for the students who are paying most of their salaries. The only way I can figure that this works is for two reasons: first, it is obviously an entrenched system, and rudeness and inefficiency can be found at every level of the institution. Second, for that reason there is little (or no) recourse for the students and even many members of the faculty, which makes them feel isolated and powerless against the system. Moreover, everyone is here to achieve so they can conceive of a better life, and a degree is a vehicle to that brighter future. Once locked in, all of the needless difficulties (administrative and otherwise) become part of the rigors of the student's path, and eventually it becomes part of the miasma that is the Hunter experience, no different from taking exams and writing papers. The unfortunate undergraduates and graduate students who have never known another college experience probably assumed that this is all there is.

I met with Rodriguez today and he told me that he had just seen an envelope from me but had not read it. (I sent it certified mail last Wednesday. It got there Friday; today is Wednesday.) I smiled and told him that everything was fine. He then informed me that he had been under pressure and that he was recovering from the flu because he had worked himself sick. He told me that he was under the gun to finish the book he had been working on and had to present a paper at a conference at Harvard in late May that he had yet to start. He then confided in me how he had gotten up at four a.m. and was exhausted trying to keep up with the demands of his job. He assured me that he would be happy to look at the thesis but could only do so once, and May 20 was the day he could. He asked me how it was coming and I explained to him how I was still struggling with chapter one, trying to appease Professor Rosencrass. He told me that he was sorry that it was taking so long. He thought that the extreme rigor Rosencrass was putting me through sounded plausible for a PhD dissertation but seemed excessive for a master's thesis. He was quick to add that he hadn't seen it, but he knew from having me as a student that I was very capable of producing quality work. I thanked him for his kind words and willingness to help.

Chapter IX

At 7:30 that evening I was to meet with Professor Rosencrass at the Roosevelt House. I was a little early getting to the Upper East Side but could not find the Roosevelt House. I don't know if he made a mistake or I wrote down the address wrong (although, admittedly, I had been there once before), but I had it written down as 68th, between Park and Madison. It's actually on 65th, and for a brief moment I sincerely wondered if Professor Rosencrass was just messing with me. When I didn't find it on 68th I asked a couple of doormen, who didn't know what I was talking about. The clock was ticking on an extremely important meeting and I started to panic. I thought I would be clever and I called 411. (I didn't have a smartphone—I had put it off, together with other luxuries, until after graduation.) They didn't have a listing for the Roosevelt House, so my next thought was to sprint back to Hunter. I arrived at the line for the help desk, panting. After I waited for the first guy, who had no idea where it was, my spirit sank. He then asked his co-greeter, who replied, "I think Sixty-Fifth and Park." Upon hearing that, I was out sprinting in my Timberland boots. I arrived there a sweaty mess, moments before Rosencrass's class let out. By the time he descended the staircase, I'd chugged most of a bottle of water, and my heart had started to slow to a normal pace. However, like times in the past, it seems that I was able to put on enough of a façade to appear quasi-normal in the face of exhaustion, or perhaps this was just how he had come to expect me.

We walked upstairs to an empty classroom and began to discuss the paper. He began going over his comments in the usual fashion, seldom allowing me to get a word in. Even when he would let me speak, he quickly cut me off. He was going on about the difficulty of the thesis. He said that many people struggle and it is hard to do a "decent job," and as soon as he said that, something within made me say that I wanted to do a "better than decent job." I was stunned to hear those words come out of my mouth and as I was hoping to withdraw that statement he jumped all over it, saying, "Yes, that's right, you want to do an excellent job." I started to realize that I had just made life harder on myself, inevitably extending the process that I had come to loathe. Instantly I began to question my belief in doing something better than average because afterward, when he's not around, I say that I don't care how well I do. I simply want this to be over.

All of these thoughts were rushing through my head as we started to go over the chapter. We both seemed content to move past pleasantries and get down to business. He said that my first chapter was getting into "reasonable shape" and that it would not need many more revisions. Although I had already revised the chapter eight times, he was still finding numerous faults. Each time he would zero in on a point and then speak about it with venom, reminiscent of how one would react if they were just insulted. When I would try to explain, he would often talk over me until I acquiesced. Before I could say anything, he would then turn to another aspect of the paper and ask me a pointed question about it. At each juncture I was still fuming because I hadn't gotten to express my previous point, so I would blurt something, which was often admittedly baldly defensive and curt. Consequently, my comments were often obtuse and did not effectively express my understanding of whatever we were talking about. He would then launch into me about the wrongness of my retort. We would continue to have similar exchanges throughout the course of our relationship.

I would inevitably revert to a familiar default mode, which was well practiced with Nora, of withdrawing from the situation, assuming that I would never get my point across so I might as well quit while I was behind. I essentially stonewalled him. I quickly realized that this approach would not help my cause and I reconsidered. I took a deep breath and became very agreeable and tried to be as receptive as possible to his advice. Although I did not completely understand all of his feedback, it appeared futile to try to explain myself. I mostly nodded and replied what I thought he would want to hear. This was how most of our meetings proceeded. Eventually he said that I shouldn't feel unusual; it is an extremely difficult process and most people struggle with it. He added that those who do not struggle mightily are the rare exceptions. When I began to allude to the fact that doing so many drafts and still being on chapter one seemed like an incredibly slow pace he told me that MA theses can take two and in some cases three years. He then reiterated that it was not an easy process. When I told him of the progress that I had made on chapters two and three he said that, after having a brief discussion about a submission schedule for the summer, it could be feasible to finish in the fall semester. He continued to say that he would like me to find a third reader for my thesis. I was initially upset by this but was careful to keep a poker face.

I could not believe that at this point in the process he was requesting a third reader for the thesis. Rodriguez had not yet read a word! This was not Rosencrass's field of expertise but he had already forced me to change my outline and had consistently found fault with my content without seeing the full product or having the requisite background to do so. Now he was asking me to find a third reader. Like everything at Hunter, there were unforeseen ways that were making the process more grueling and my ability to finish in a reasonable amount of time less possible. I could not believe what I was hearing.

When I started to question this, Rosencrass cut the meeting short by saying that he had to meet a former student for a dinner appointment. I begrudgingly thanked him for his time and we descended the stairs together making somewhat awkward small talk. When we reached the fancy lobby of the Roosevelt House there was an attractive young woman standing there. He introduced us and I noticed that she had some sort of Eastern European accent. He said that Annabel had spent some time showing his daughter around Paris when his daughter had been studying abroad there. He said that she was a former student of his and he told her that I was currently working on an MA thesis with him. He joked that I was probably ready to rip his head off now, after he had painstakingly corrected my work. I didn't expect him to be so candid and found myself momentarily lost for words. As the silence between us became more palpable I felt that I needed to say something and I smiled, looked into Annabel's eyes, and said, "He is meticulous." She quickly replied, "He's horrendous!" I was struck by her words, but I didn't want to linger. I told them that I didn't want to hold them any longer. As I left, Professor Rosencrass said, "Take it easy, Loren," and I replied that I would not—I'd be working hard.

Professor Rosencrass recommended I attend the conference at NYU in early April, which, along with the meetings, was the reason why I was in New York City on this occasion. The conference was free of charge as long as one registered in advance and it seemed like an excellent opportunity to explore the state of the field and learn from some of its most prestigious professors. Greg Grandin, the closest thing to a celebrity in the field, was one of the keynote speakers. I had read a couple of Grandin's books and had tremendous respect for the compelling quality of his recounting of history.

There were professors from a number of high-caliber institutions such as Yale, NYU, and Wake Forest presenting papers on their particular areas of interest, which all fell under the larger theme of "American (Inter) Dependencies: New Perspectives on Capitalism and Empire 1898–1959." They would present their work and a panel would respond to it. Then the audience would have an opportunity to ask questions to the presenters, who sat on their own panel, usually in groups of three. The two-day affair would conclude with a plenary panel with heavy hitters like Paul Kramer, Greg Grandin, and Barbara Weinstein.

When I arrived, I was nervous. I was exhausted because I had attempted to read the hundreds of pages of pre-submitted journal articles and book chapters that were not released until what seemed a very short time before the conference. I watched and listened as the presenting professors arrived. Amazingly, although they were from different universities, most of them greeted each other like long-lost friends, or at least with some friendly professional familiarity. Once the conference commenced, I was shocked again that only a handful of the attendees were not directly involved in the conference.

During the second panel, which was titled "Producing Economic Knowledge," the presenters expounded on a wide range of fascinating topics rooted in the papers they were presenting. Much of the discussion was admittedly over my head and I was racing to write down jargon and books that I should explore. However, there were several historical themes with which I was familiar and books they mentioned that I had read during my odyssey at Hunter. One theme that stuck out for me was that many historians had done research at the Rockefeller Foundation. I had always been skeptical of the heavy involvement of the Rockefellers in historical research. It was a theme that I had run up against time and again as I delved deeper into the history of US–Latin American relations. The David Rockefeller Center for Latin American Studies (DRCLAS) at Harvard University was one of several ways the Rockefellers had been able to influence Americans' perceptions of Latin American history. It was perplexing to me that the Rockefeller family, who were historical actors, could also shape how the history was being recorded and recounted. Therefore, I asked the presenters: How could the Rockefeller Foundation, where they were doing a portion of their research, not shape their narratives and our perception of history? This was met with some astonishment, but the panelists seemed like kind people and they did their best to answer me. They said that they could only do their best as historians to analyze the information as objectively as possible. One jokingly added that the free meals in the cafeteria of the Rockefeller Center were probably responsible for countless footnotes.

After the panel there was a break and I ran into one of the event's coordinators, Augustine Sedgewick of the University of Toronto.

From his incisive introduction it was obvious that he was a highly intelligent man who took his job seriously, but his solemn professionalism was balanced by a playful, razor-sharp wit. He complimented me on my question and encouraged me to participate more. He asked me where I studied and seemed deeply interested in my career path and ideas. He treated me like a fellow colleague, something that was a rare occurrence at Hunter, where I often felt like a nuisance. As the conference unfolded I asked one more question, which was also well received. Several of the presenting professors went out of their way to speak with me and I felt that I was making some solid connections.

Many people were in and out during the day, but the number of audience members hovered around twenty. By the second day, there were times when I was one of only a couple of people who were not part of the conference. The numbers were highest for the plenary panel, at about seventy-five to one hundred people. The discussion at the plenary panel was riveting and important and the participants were brilliant—they made it well worth sitting through the entire two-day conference. After the plenary panel there was a mixer with wine and cheese. I spoke to several of the professors, and to many I gave well-deserved compliments on their work. Nearly all of them were very cordial and asked me trenchant questions about my thesis and my course of study. It felt very different from most of my interactions at Hunter and all of my interactions with Eduardo Caraja and Professor Rosencrass. I left feeling elated and I wrote emails to all of the professors I had spoken with at the conference. Each of them replied and kindly said that they hoped to stay in touch and wished me well on my thesis. To my surprise and delight, even Greg Grandin replied to my email, saying, "Keep me posted on what you decide to do!" It was an eye-opening experience and a stark contrast to my experiences at Hunter. Unfortunately, the high of the conference soon burned off and I was back in Hunter's merciless thrall.

The following journal entry contains brief reflections after a particularly difficult phone discussion about my thesis.

June 16, 2014

I just got off the phone with Professor Rosencrass. He was supposed to call me after a luncheon, which he estimated would end around 2:30. I spent the entire day preparing for the meeting. He called me around 3:40. He did apologize for calling me late and I responded with my ready phrase: "I know you are a busy man and I appreciate your making time for me." He was, as usual, very hard on my work. He would repeatedly talk over me as I was trying to respond to his points or simply ask for clarification. He would ask pointed questions, often as I was in the process of explaining myself, and then he would cut me off and go on to something else. It was more difficult to follow, I imagined, than being a drunken spectator trying to follow a little white ball at a world-class ping-pong match. At one point the communication was so disjointed, due largely to his domineering style, that he cut me off in the midst of explaining why I had used a particular source and asked me if I knew what a primary source was. It was obviously demeaning and offensive, but I was too busy trying to keep up with the onslaught to notice more than a brief sting. He can't help but rip apart everything I do and he never will tell me that anything I produce has any merit; it is simply "acceptable" or "not too bad." It makes me feel worthless as a writer and helpless in my thesis process.

I can't believe this process has been drawn out for so long, and it continues to get more painful as I go along. While he was grilling me on my lack of primary sources I wanted to tell him about the countless hours in libraries, historical archives, on the phone, and retrieving and printing stacks of primary sources for my previous thesis, without including everything that had gone into this one. But I knew that it would get me nowhere.

A large part of the problem with Hunter is that the situation is changing, so it is hard for me to be able to know or produce what they want me to. I don't have the time to go down each corridor of study because I am constantly trying to adapt to their criteria. For the first time in speaking with my Hunter professors, I was unable to control my temper and I was short with him. At times I could not help but be contentious and also more assertive. When I did assert my point of view, he often agreed with me, mostly begrudgingly. But he was quick to add some other point of his to undermine me, seemingly out of spite. Overall, he seemed to care little about what I had to say.

Academia has once again taken most of the joy out of writing for me. My life feels once again tainted with frustration, inadequacy, etc. Perhaps the most frustrating part is that this is not the life I want to lead. Many times I have thought that I should simply walk away. Unfortunately, now it seems as if I have passed the point of no return, even though the whole process feels so dead to me, and is a source of endless aggravation. It seems that no matter what I do it is never enough; no matter how many hours I put in it is still impossible for me to do the right thing. The entire process has been painfully slow and it inhibits my life in many ways: financially, intellectually, creatively, etc. This process has had me in a holding pattern in many facets of my life for years.

JUNE 17, 2014

I now see why students go to extremes over academic angst, like shooting up schools and committing suicide, because aside from being highly competitive, it is an all-or-nothing pursuit: you either graduate or you don't. People who find themselves in positions like mine realize that they are powerless to do anything. The feeling of powerlessness deforms some into performing an extreme action that allows them to continue to be in control of something. It has become exhausting because I can't help but think about an end to this situation every day. I need this to end as soon as possible.

JUNE 18, 2014

Today has been another chapter in the hole of depression I have been living in. I have been feeling sad and worthless again, a state of mind my mother says has been built through years of mistreatment at Hunter combined with various other external factors. The depression is triggered now by Professor Rosencrass because I have little contact with Hunter besides him. It has been an extremely tumultuous stretch for me and his abrasive style triggers all of these memories and negative feelings from my past. It has been a very odd time. I cannot get beyond this period in my life.

JUNE 19, 2014

One of the most aggravating parts of this process is that every time I have an unsatisfactory meeting with Professor Rosencrass it unleashes this flood of emotions that sends me down a spiral staircase back into that dark place I hate. When this happens it incapacitates me and I can't get done what I need to. I then spend the day trying to build myself back up, whereas if I wasn't dealing with this awful component I would be much happier and consequently more productive. Ultimately it makes this task, and my life in general, feel even more impossible, which increasingly fills me with despair.

Chapter X

With no certainty that I would ever finish my thesis, I decided to quit. After two years of work on this thesis I had not produced an acceptable first chapter. We simply moved on to my second chapter as my first was "almost acceptable." I had then revised my new second chapter a couple of times and it continued to be a war of attrition. When we finished the discussion on June 16, 2014, Rosencrass reluctantly agreed to look at the third chapter because I assured him that it would put the second chapter into the proper context, something that he said the second chapter was lacking. When I hung up the phone I felt awful. After almost six years of being enrolled at Hunter, with graduate school as the main focus of my life, there still was no guarantee that I would finish. I was infuriated and needed to step away from the situation. I spent the rest of the summer away from my studies at Hunter and day by day, a little at a time, my depression started to lift.

Looking back on the following journal entry, I guess this is when the decision was made:

October 9, 2014

The entire thesis process has become a malignant tumor in my life and I believe that time away from it will allow me to replace the futile struggle with something positive and more fulfilling. Time away has been glorious. I still feel behind in many facets of my life and I know that I have numerous loose ends, which I have neglected, but I can work on them. I now understand how completely exhausted I was with the situation at Hunter and that it was transforming me into a person I don't want to be. It is so pleasant to have time to work and still enjoy life some without my duties at Hunter hanging over my head.

By October I still had not heard anything from Professor Rosencrass about my third chapter, which he'd said he would get back to me about in June. Obviously he had a minuscule amount of interest in my situation compared to everything that I had invested in this degree and what it meant for me to finish. It was at this time that I began realize that he really didn't care whether I finished or not.

My cousin was living in Palermo, Sicily, at the time, and she said that if I wanted to take a chance I could move in with her and she could find me some work as an ESL tutor. For more than six years I had shaped my life around my education at Hunter College and eschewed many other opportunities due to my commitment to my graduate studies. I kept operating under the belief that if I just pushed a little harder, worked longer, I would be done. It was as if I was running a marathon, and each time I could see the finish line it was pulled back from me until the finish line became nothing more than a mirage. I had given so much I had nothing left to give. I realized that I was much happier away from the work, and that this degree had come to dominate nearly every facet of my life.

In late October I made the difficult decision to call it quits, and I sent Professor Rosencrass a very simple email telling him not to bother to look at the third chapter because I was suspending my studies indefinitely.

He swiftly responded, claiming that he had read the third chapter "several months ago," but that it seemed futile to send his comments since I had made this surprising decision. He then wished me luck, saying that I would "find interesting things to do," and added, "I am sure you will work hard at them."

Professor Rodriguez never had the chance to read a word of my thesis. After more than six years and tens of thousands of dollars, I finally walked away. I decided that I needed to do something different and I didn't want to be a part of what the people at Hunter were trying to make me. The difficult decision then was what to do next. I had compiled hundreds of pages of notes and ramblings about my time at Hunter, with the vague idea that I would perhaps publish it one day when I had received my degree. I decided that I would not want this to happen to anyone else and that I had a duty to at least inform future students with my story.

I also began drafting a letter. At that point I was not sure who to send the letter to, but I knew that it had to be sent to someone important at Hunter. After months of working on the letter, trying to strike the difficult balance between including what had happened to me and brevity, I produced a ten-page letter detailing my travails. I had several people close to the situation look at it until we agreed that it was the best I could do. In the letter I was as specific as I could be about the details of my experience, and at the end I demanded that they repay me every cent that I gave the institution, which I thought was the least they could do. (The letter is included in the appendix.)

I wasn't sure where to send it so I asked Professor Harvey Lebowitz for advice. He recommended that I send it to Provost Morta Derewitz first. But "don't be surprised if she doesn't answer you," he warned. On January 5, 2015, I sent her the letter via certified mail. On January 8, it was signed for by someone else in her office. By this time I had already been making arrangements to move to Sicily. I planned to stop in New York City on my way to Europe to meet with some people who I believed I could trust to get advice on the Hunter situation. By the time I left, I still had not heard back from Provost Derewitz.

On February 5, 2015, I met with Professor Lebowitz, the only professor I'd studied under at Hunter with whom I felt I had a genuine connection that stretched beyond the classroom. We met for coffee near the Lincoln Center in Manhattan. After we exchanged a little small talk, we got down to Hunter business. He told me how he had been pushed from the program after his contract was not renewed. He tried multiple times to contact Hunter president Terry Daub, and she continually ignored his emails. She simply ignored him until he left. He told me other horror stories about professors I had never met who were pushed from their positions because, like him, they were perceived to be aligned with other members of the department or for various other reasons. The reasons were solely political and had nothing to do with academics.

As we spoke more I began to feel a little better, because I stopped feeling alone. My particular situation there made me feel so isolated, and because it was such a large part of my life it had warped my sense of reality. It was so long and confusing that I was unsure whether all of these seemingly unconscionable things that were happening at the hands of these academics were real or whether I was distorting the facts in my mind.

On February 26, I sent Provost Derewitz an email to follow up. After hearing nothing for over two months, I followed Lebowitz's advice and sent the letter to President Daub on March 10. It was signed for by someone in her office a few days later. On April 3, as I was just about to send Terry Daub a follow-up email, a certified letter arrived from Morta Derewitz.

The letter was filled with lies and inconsistencies from everyone who had been involved in the situation. There were no apologies, just a cold and businesslike tone. She ended the letter with this frustratingly unrepentant statement: "Unfortunately, by deciding, of your own volition, to leave the program, despite the attention you have received from the Department, I regret to conclude, with the Department, that you are not in a position to earn the MA in History at Hunter College."

I was not surprised that they put the entire responsibility on me. What did surprise me a little was that everyone involved who was questioned about the situation at least exaggerated the truth, and many flat-out lied. Some of the things they said about the chronology were impossible and others were simply not true. The letter was poorly written and littered with inconsistencies and untruths.

One of the glaring inconsistencies was with regard to my experience with Professor Caraja. Provost Derewitz interviewed Professor Caraja, who told her that we met three times for meetings that lasted "at least two hours." Then the letter said that I had "weekly opportunities to visit Professor Caraja during office hours." Derewitz wrote that I had "dropped by at the end of office hours" and that he only had "10-15 minutes" before he had to get ready for his evening class. She said I was able to review the exam for more than an hour. She said that I would then be able to return to study the exam again during office hours, and finished by ominously saying, "you did not."

I have already stated my version of these events, which makes some of these wild claims impossible. He said that I had "dropped by at the end of office hours" for a meeting, which I had set up months in advance, and he had told me that he was completely unavailable for the rest of the time I was in New York City. I did not have "weekly opportunities to visit Professor Caraja during office hours" because I lived four hundred miles away. I had moved home because I could not afford to continue to live in the city while pursuing the degree.

Let's consider for a moment that their erroneous claim that we met three times for two hours is correct. This means that, including the hour of review I had for the exam, I had a net seven hours with this professor to work on my two exams and my thesis. I no longer have access to all of the financial records from this period of my life, but a low-end estimate of the cost for maintaining my matriculation, paying for a thesis (it should be pointed out that I did not pay for the thesis until my second thesis with Professor Rosencrass in 2013), and miscellaneous fees paid to Hunter (not including the money paid to travel four hundred miles each way to the school and other related expenses) is at least $1,400. This means that they were charging me roughly $200 per hour to sit and have these discussions with someone who ultimately did not believe that working with me was worth his time.

When I sent the response to Professor Lebowitz, he was alarmed when he read the letter. He said that he knew Derewitz's writing style and that she was not the one who had written the letter. He gave me a stern warning that this was written by a lawyer. He suggested that I simply walk away and never look back. Derewitz has since been rewarded for this and other deeds on behalf of the administration at Hunter with a new position and a raise to her six-figure salary.

I received the letter and response in Italy and was unsure what to do next. For years, as I had been working multiple jobs and working on my personal writing in addition to my degree, many people told me, "Just work a little harder and you'll get over the hump." As a result, I was constantly telling myself that if I just pushed a little harder, got up earlier, put in more hours, and hired the right editor to coach me through my thesis I would be able to finish the degree and move on with my life. But as the finish line kept being pulled away from me, I had become more and more burned out. By the end of my efforts on my second thesis, I had gotten to the point that I could not concentrate on my academic work for more than fifteen minutes at a time.

Having my thesis constantly ripped apart, combined with other problems I was having outside of academia, was making me feel worthless. My entire life was meeting deadlines, working, jumping through hoops, and doing everything within my power to focus and produce. Looking back on it, during the last few years I was pursuing the degree, my lifestyle was unsustainable and it was sapping my energy and causing my mental and physical health to deteriorate. I could not understand this when I was mired in the situation, but the letter from Provost Derewitz was simply a gravestone on my time at Hunter. I was officially done.

What they took from me was a sense of certainty in my choice to further my education. My education through high school was dissatisfying enough to make me question attending college but my family encouraged me and many of my friends were doing the same. I gradually settled into a fairly serious academic career because I had greater control over what I could study. As a result, my education focused on topics I was legitimately interested in. I was an above-average student for my entire academic career. But by the time I had finished my bachelor's degree I was exhausted by the academic setting and I itched to do something new—most of all to see the world. I thought I would never return to school. When I made it to Hunter, I was excited by the new challenges. I did the finest academic work of my entire career in my graduate school coursework because I was more engaged than ever.

Conclusion

Looking back on my academic career, it is clear that I became trapped in a system. There were moments when I felt wise and powerful, living a life that promised something better. But most of the time I was working and trying to fight off a deep-seated sadness. Some of the best moments in my life are when I feel the love of people I care about and the connectivity I have with everything. These feelings have nothing to do with academia. There are times in my life when the possibilities seem endless and my existence feels like the pinnacle of it all. These times never have anything to do with Hunter College.

I had chosen to return to academia because I loved aspects of college and yearned to teach. My experience at Hunter completely deterred me from this path. At Hunter there was a cold competitiveness and a palpable apathy from many of the students and the majority of the professors. There were a few professors (mostly adjuncts) I had in my time at Hunter who I could tell had a genuine passion for teaching and took an interest in their students as individuals. Generally, those were the professors who were the most frustrated with the way Hunter had treated them as employees and with the barriers that the corporatized bureaucratic structure erected between students, instructors, and education.

Hunter College raised the stress level for nearly everyone involved during my time there. I believe that the unnecessary pressure and stress retarded my progress because humans don't learn best when they are in a constant state of panic. Many bureaucratic problems and nonacademic stresses at Hunter made my learning experience more difficult than it should have been.

During my time at Hunter, I was rarely inspired to learn by anyone other than myself. Rather than focus on my interests, as I tried to do with the independent study and my theses, my advisors focused more on jumping through administrative hoops, testing, and making the program as rigorous as possible. Time and again I would hear about the high standards of my professors, but never about their passion for teaching or their excitement about my passion to learn. It was more about breaking me down than building me up as a student and as a person. I know that many will contend that at the graduate level you are an adult and don't need coddling, and I agree to a large extent. However, I never sought to be coddled. I simply sought an education in pursuit of a credential I would need in order to embark on a career path.

I was routinely stretched to breaking point. My mother (a licensed mental health therapist) told me that Hunter College began to trigger symptoms of PTSD in me. Education was not at the heart of my experience at Hunter College. My situation there was horrible enough for me to give up my dream of teaching at the college level, and it has transformed me into someone totally different than I was when I entered. I wish, if nothing else, that no other student will have to endure what I did at Hunter.

When I visited NYC on my way to Italy after my decision to leave

Hunter College, I decided to take the 4 train to Lehman one last time to thank and say good-bye to Professor Rodriguez. He was his usual kind self and he spoke to me freely about my difficult decision. I thought about his last words all the way back to my hotel room. He had told me that anyone who spoke with me for a few minutes could see that I was passionate about learning and that he was ashamed because "we have failed you."

Although my experience at Hunter is extreme, it is not without precedent. Hunter does many things poorly, and unfortunately I don't believe that the institution is an outlier. I have tried to do my part to shed light on the situation in the hopes of helping other students who are caught in a similar vortex.

I have come to see the academic world differently than when I first enrolled in grad school. The conversations I have had with students and professors, combined with my experience, have shown me the darker side of higher education. The trend of corporatization tends to undermine the voice of students and some members of the faculty by placing an inordinate amount of power in the hands of administrators. As a result, higher education in this nation is, in some cases, run like a business. But it should not be operated in this fashion, because an education is more than a transaction.

At Hunter the administration created a culture so insular that it prohibits healthy scrutiny and, in my case, recourse. I would have benefitted from an external review by an objective party. In the future, students should be encouraged to come forward and contribute to a dialogue about ways to reform a system that disconnects professionals and students. There must be more oversight, not only of the professors, but of the bureaucrats who are supposed to be watching them.

The students and adjunct professors should have more say in the direction of education. While there are many professors who take an interest in the development of their students, many others could benefit from approaching their jobs with a deeper level of humanity. Collusion between departments and administrations should be routinely inspected. I hope this account contributes in a small way to a broader dialogue, which is long overdue.

Appendix

Letter from Loren Mayshark to Joshua Rosencrass

Loren Mayshark
4585 Sunrise Drive
Bemus Point, New York 14712

Professor Joshua Rosencrass, PhD
C/o Hunter College History Department
695 Park Avenue,
New York, New York 10065

October 22, 2011

Dear Professor Rosencrass,

Thank you for offering to meet with Professor Belview and with me to discuss my future. After pondering my current situation I wanted to communicate some of my concerns.

I was first invited into the MA program as a non-matriculated Latin American history student three and a half years ago. At that time, and subsequently when I was accepted into the program, I had the understanding that there was a viable Latin American studies concentration at Hunter as listed in the catalogue. When I learned that this was not actually the case and had already completed several courses, I was appreciative that Hunter College was going to accommodate me by providing the guidance and requirements to complete my degree. I was told to wait for Professor Regresso who was on sabbatical and had not yet joined the faculty at Hunter.

In the interim, unfortunately, no one was able to direct me as to the course work requisites because the Latin American program was being reconstructed. I was told to "just continue taking classes," initially by Professor Wallace and later by you. Throughout the program I maintained a 3.6 GPA. More importantly, all the courses represented the rigor of Hunter College by requiring challenging papers and examinations. I was pleased to receive positive feedback from my professors with regard to my papers, my exams, and my grasp of the material. I received verbal and written endorsements. I had every reason to be encouraged by my progress.

When Professor Regresso joined the faculty, I was beginning my final semester of course work. She explained she could not help me towards the completion of my degree because my thesis is about U.S. Latino labor, which fell outside her area of expertise. In order to complete my degree, Professor Regresso recommended that I try to work with Professor Caraja and you were kind enough to aid me in that endeavor.

Professor Eduardo Caraja consented to act as my advisor for the comprehensive exam. He would also be the primary reader of my thesis with the stipulation that I wait to complete it in the spring semester of 2012. I was immensely grateful to him for his willingness to work with me; particularly since he is currently working on his sabbatical project and has little time. Unfortunately, I never had an opportunity to take a class from him, because his classes were only offered after I completed my coursework. Therefore, he does not know my work.

On December 14th of 2010, he assigned a daunting 38 books, but I managed to read 31 books in ten weeks. Professor Caraja could only afford to give me approximately 4 hours of instruction prior to the test that I elected to take on February 25, 2011. After the first test, Professor Caraja was able to give me only 10 minutes of feedback before I took the second exam. It is my understanding that comprehensive exams are based on a student's cumulative knowledge of the scholarship within their field of study over a period of their entire graduate career. I took all the courses pertaining to Latin American studies, of which there were only three. Furthermore, I chose topics pertinent to my interests in Latin American history for my projects in other classes, namely Modern Intellectual History and Historical Methods. Moreover, I made a special effort to commute to Lehman College to study U.S./Latin American Relations with Professor Rodriquez. While these classes were valuable for general background, only two of the books I read were included in the 38 assigned for the comprehensive exam.

I realize, with gratitude, that the faculty is trying to help me design a tailored program. I am trying to master vast amounts of new material in a very short period of time. Unfortunately, my current dilemma is that if I fail on a third occasion, I will be out of the program. Additionally, I am concerned about the time limits of the program and I am worried about having ample opportunity to assimilate so much new material to meet Professor Caraja's expectations on the test and still do a good job on the thesis.

I believe that I have been a sincerely dedicated student. I have never received a failing score on a test during my entire graduate or undergraduate career. I passed the language comprehensive on my first try. My perseverance towards the degree is exemplified by the fact that I had emergency spinal cord surgery in the middle of my second semester. In spite of a grueling recovery, I only missed three classes and completed the courses with an A- and a B+ that semester.

At present, I am working in Western New York. I live more than

400 miles away from Hunter where I am doing research for my thesis on the history of Latino labor in this region. It is difficult for me to get time off from my jobs because I have had to negotiate so often with my supervisors to meet the requirements of my studies. If it is possible, would you be able to correspond with me via a letter or e-mail? I would very much appreciate it. Thank you for considering this. However, if this does not seem possible, I will make every effort to travel to Hunter.

Respectfully,
Loren Mayshark

Letter from Loren Mayshark to Morta Derewitz

Loren Mayshark
4585 Sunrise Drive
Bemus Point, NY 14712

Dr. Morta Derewitz, Provost and Vice President of Academic Affairs
HUNTER COLLEGE
695 Park Ave
NY, NY 10065

January 5, 2015

Dear Dr. Derewitz,

My name is Loren Mayshark and I am writing this letter to inform you about an injustice levied upon me during my time at Hunter College. I am writing you in hopes that we can rectify this situation. I am requesting a full reimbursement of the funds I have rendered to Hunter in pursuit of the MA in History, which I have made every serious attempt to obtain. Below is a description of my experience at Hunter. After six years of paying money to your institution, maintaining a 3.6 GPA and carrying out the academic rigors of Hunter College, I still do not have any concrete guarantee of receiving a degree.

Four years after obtaining a B.A. in History from Manhattanville College and spending time in South America, I was accepted as a non-matriculated student into Hunter's Graduate Master's program for the Fall Semester of 2008 in History. There is no doubt that Hunter has a prestigious academic reputation. I was fortunate to encounter some faculty who were inspiring scholars, encouraging, and gifted with students. However, in my experience and that of many people I spoke with at the school, both students and faculty members, the bureaucratic morass at the college has been off-putting and difficult, and in my case inordinately severe.

Given my interest in Latin American studies and my proficiency in Spanish, I was motivated to gain a degree in Latin American History. The department at Hunter was geared toward U.S. and European History, but this was unclear at my time of acceptance as a non-matriculated student. Unfortunately, the fact only came to light after I was accepted into the program. Despite the emphasis on U.S. and European History, Hunter's catalogue also lists programs in Jewish, Latin American, African History and a few others. When I entered Hunter, the program requirements, aside from coursework, were a thesis and two comprehensive exams: one for foreign language proficiency and the other for cumulative knowledge in a given field of history (for me that was Latin America).

When I began attending, I was living in Southold on Long Island and made the 2.5 hour (each way) weekly commute to Manhattan for my first class, "Democracy and Development in Latin America and Africa." In my first semester, I met with the academic advisor for the program, Professor Hannah Wallace, and inquired about gaining full acceptance into the MA History program with a concentration in Latin American History. Her advice was that I focus on getting into the MA History program first before fixing on my specific interests. She recommended that I re-apply and sign up for more classes, maintain a B or better and that "would likely lead to entrance as a fully matriculated student." I received a B in "Democracy and Development in Latin America and Africa." I re-applied, was denied, but I concurrently signed up for two more classes, "Modern Mexican History" and "History and Memory."

I moved to Astoria, Queens to focus on my studies. Toward the end of my second semester, I had an unexpected life-altering event. I lost feeling in my extremities and was subjected to a nine-hour emergency spinal cord surgery. In spite of a grueling recovery, and encouragement by my two professors to take incompletes, I only missed two class sessions in each course and completed all coursework on time. I am including this information as an indication of my dedication and passion for the subject matter. I received an A- and a B+ that semester. I lost my job because of my physical constraints (I wore a Miami J brace for four months and was compromised physically for a long period of time). Since I had not been accepted into the program, and I had taken the maximum amount of non-matriculated classes, I had to wait a semester before I could re-apply. Meanwhile, during that late summer and fall, while I was waiting, I took some Spanish classes at the Brecht Forum and writing classes at the New York Writer's Workshop and the Gotham Writer's Workshop to hone the skills necessary to complete the degree.

Finally, two fees, living expenses, and tuition later, I was accepted into the program as a fully matriculated student for the spring semester of 2010. In that semester I passed the language comprehensive exam on the first attempt. Unfortunately I had to move out of the city for financial reasons and endured a long commute from Derby, Connecticut. I took three classes and received high marks in all of them, giving me a total of eighteen graduate credits. Meanwhile, I met with the new Graduate Advisor, Professor Rosencrass, who had taken Professor Wallace's place. When I asked about the Latin American History degree, Prof. Rosencrass responded by saying that he was not aware of the program. I pointed out that it was listed in the college course catalogue and Professor Rosencrass looked this information up on the computer, in front of me, and it was confirmed. He said that he would agree to find a tenable course of study for me, which would include all of the classes I had taken prior and all of the ones I was currently enrolled in. He then advised me to continue taking courses until the arrival of Professor Regresso, a full-time Latin American history professor Hunter had hired. She was expected to arrive in fall of 2010, after her sabbatical from Columbia University ended. I began a protracted email correspondence with Professor Regresso. Ultimately, she recommended that I take her lone graduate class on Colonial Latin American History in the Fall Semester of 2010 and meet with her then. Moreover, in my final semester I made a special effort to commute to Lehman College to take a class on the History of U.S./Latin American Relations with Professor Rodriquez. At that point it seemed that every move I made at the school was a bureaucratic headache and that each member of the faculty had part of the answer I was seeking but no one had the entire answer. However, with the expectation of Professor Regresso's arrival my prospects seemed to be improving.

When Professor Regresso finally became available to meet with me, I was in the last semester of coursework, leaving only the thesis and final exam standing between me and the degree, pending good grades in the classes I was taking. In the meeting, Professor Regresso explained that she would not feel comfortable "staking her credentials" on a comprehensive exam for me because Hunter did not have the faculty to provide sufficient coursework to prepare me for such an exam. Moreover, she told me that my thesis proposal, which was on Latino migrant labor in the U.S., fell outside of her expertise and she advised me to find another primary reader for the thesis. When I returned to Professor Rosencrass with this information, he told me, as Professor Regresso had mentioned, to consult another newly added faculty member, Professor Enrique Caraja.

Professor Caraja consented to act as advisor for the comprehensive exam and to be the primary reader of the thesis if I would wait until the spring of 2012 to complete the thesis, due to a sabbatical that he was taking to work on a book. I was immensely grateful to him for his willingness to work with me; particularly since he was working on his sabbatical project and had little time. Unfortunately, I never had an opportunity to take a class from him, because he offered graduate classes only after I had completed my coursework. Therefore, he did not know my work.

At the end of the semester, I had to move home to Western New York due to dire finances resulting from my injury and loss of work. On December 14th of 2010, he assigned a daunting list of 38 books to prepare for my exam. I managed to read 31 books in ten weeks. Professor Caraja could only afford to give me approximately 4 hours of instruction prior to the test. I elected to take the exam on February 25, 2011. After approximately one month of waiting, I was informed that I failed the exam, the only time I had failed in my entire academic career. Immediately after the test, I began to work on a thesis proposal that I sent to Professor Caraja.

In May, I again traveled over 400 miles in order to speak with Professor Caraja, in a pre-arranged meeting, about both my thesis and my exam. Professor Caraja told me that he was very busy, so busy that he could only meet with me for forty-five minutes and that he had no other time to meet with me for the rest of the week while I was in New York. He then informed me that he would not be able to meet with me again before the following January as he would be on sabbatical for the summer and fall. So outside of a forty-five minute window in mid-May, I would have zero time to review my test with him before the retake in September. He agreed that he would glance at some pages of my thesis if sent to him before May 21st, but then he would be completely uninvolved with the paper until late January or early February of 2012. He then chided me by saying that I was at a disadvantage for choosing a course of study which was unorthodox and reminded me that it is difficult to work with a professor without taking a class from him. I agreed that I would have enjoyed and benefited from taking a class from him but since he didn't teach a graduate class at the school until after I had taken the entirety of my courses, this was impossible. So after the preliminary discussion on his unavailability, I had thirty-five minutes to go over my thesis and another ten minutes to go over my three-hour test which I had spent months studying for. The entire session felt dizzyingly rushed.

First, I was told that I failed my exam because my introductory paragraphs were not specific enough and I was told that I couldn't sustain my arguments. Then he attacked the technical nature of my writing and said that he expected more from a graduate student. When I pressed him for examples, he pointed out a couple of two-sentence paragraphs, which he said were completely unacceptable at the graduate level. He said that he expected more from a graduate student and implied that I had slipped through the program until meeting someone with his serious academic ability and prowess. I am sure the other professors who had given me an accumulated GPA of 3.6, at the graduate level, would disagree. Answering three essay questions with handwritten responses on everything and anything from thirty-eight new books is a daunting task. During the four hours of instruction Professor Caraja had never explained what the grading criteria would be and I was never able to find a concrete explanation on how the exams are specifically scored. When I inquired about the methods of their evaluation, he became incensed. No, he could not tell me what the specifics of the grading criteria were. When I gave him a puzzled look as I was trying to understand why I had failed this exam, he coldly replied that his standards are "extremely high" and yet again alluded to the fact that we hadn't worked together and added that if I didn't want to continue with him he would understand. I knew that there was no other person in the entire program who could oversee my thesis or exam so it would be impossible to work with anyone else. After completing the coursework successfully, waiting for Professor Regresso's return to no avail, and having Professor Rosencrass suggest Professor Caraja as my only alternative at Hunter, I felt compelled to be conciliatory and promised him I would work even harder and try to do better on the second exam attempt.

After Professor Caraja's brief and severe explanation of my thesis and the reasons I failed the exam, I was told that I could look over my test. However, I could not remove my exam from his sight: "Hunter Policy." He then told me that I was to go stand outside of his office while he locked the door behind him and went to the bathroom. Although this was a demeaning start to the session, I was anxious to spend all the time reviewing the test. When he returned, I was given the exam, five full blue booklets in all. I hurriedly began jotting down as many notes as possible pertaining to the three questions. Literally about five minutes into reading the exam, he told me that he had a "meeting with the department chair in ten minutes." When I began to tell him that I was still going over the test, he told me that I already had taken more than an hour of his time. So I shut my mouth, knowing that the clock was ticking and arguing would get me nowhere. I rushed and wrote down as many notes as I could, but before I knew it, my time was up and I was only beginning to review my second essay. As I walked into the elevator, I felt cheated and insignificant. I began to worry, knowing that I would have to prepare for the exam again with very little feedback on how I was to improve my work. It felt worse knowing that the only person who could instruct me would be unreachable. I felt completely alone and vulnerable, unsure how I was supposed to proceed.

I returned home dejected and frustrated. However, I immediately returned to my thesis research and worked frantically to produce as many pages as I could. I sent him about a dozen pages by his May 21st deadline and I did not hear from him for weeks. Finally, on July 27th he sent me an edited version of the dozen pages that I had sent him for my thesis. In an attached letter he stated, "You are certainly on the right track and there are some good moments in the material you sent me. Of course, as you are well aware, you have a great deal of work to do." I knew how much toil lay ahead, but I was determined to finish.

I read through his comments and digested them, but I did not have the luxury of applying those suggestions to my work because it was now already early August and the retake of my exam was less than two months away. I knew I had to put the thesis aside and focus on my exam. This time the preparation was torturous. I was overwhelmed by the constant work on the exam and thesis. The futility of studying the books I had read with minimal input from a professor and the fear of not really knowing his expectations, which were not communicated to me in any form, made me doubt whether my efforts alone would be enough to be successful. I had no choice but to trudge forward and depend on my past academic successes. I still wanted to complete this degree.

In order to take the exam again in the Fall Semester, I had to pay another $300 to maintain my matriculation. I then retook the test and failed for a second time. I had studied for the test indefatigably. I was completely destroyed after the second test and so was my faith in Hunter. After more than three years my time at Hunter started to feel like an unending cycle of fees, setbacks and disappointments.

It was Hunter policy that if an individual fails the Comprehensive Exam twice they can be expelled from the program. I wrote a sober letter to Professor Belview (Chair of the History Department at the time) and Professor Rosencrass explaining the situation. In response they proposed that the three of us sit down and discuss my circumstances, because, as they said, "you are a good student." I traveled back for another meeting on November 18, 2011.

When I met with them, I was informed that Professor Caraja claimed that his willingness to advise the thesis was contingent on my performance on the test (as I have mentioned, this was not the case) and as a result, he decided he would no longer work with me. In the wake of this decision, the chair of the department, Professor Belview, and Professor Rosencrass, proposed that I take the U.S. comprehensive exam (which would entail reading the entire curriculum of books that the U.S. concentration Master's History students read) and finding a new primary reader for an entirely different thesis. This was obviously unrealistic and would have meant a minimum of another two years of study without the guarantee of a degree and another move back to live in NYC, which I could no longer afford.

I explored the possibility of transferring, but I would only be able to transfer a maximum of twelve credits of the twenty-seven I had earned, even if I transferred to another CUNY school, and I would still have to do a thesis and perhaps another exam. I considered contacting the Chancellor of CUNY or even getting legal help. The MA History program with a concentration on Latin America, as stated in the course catalog, was nonexistent. Also, although I had been told to take courses, which I successfully completed, I had been given minimal instruction on the cumulative material for the specific exam for which I was being held accountable.

On 6/3/12, I received an email from Professor Rosencrass telling me that Hunter was changing the program and they no longer required a comprehensive exam in order to receive a degree. After I had failed twice, they were doing away with the requisite; I was shocked. Professor

Rosencrass advised me to find a primary and secondary reader for a new thesis. Normally, one would be thrilled with such news, but given my history with Hunter, I received the news with cautious enthusiasm. I still entertained the idea of teaching at the college level, so I decided to press on. Despite my misgivings about further financial and emotional demands, I decided to return to Hunter in good faith.

In spite of the many hours of work I had done on the original thesis, I would return and pick a new thesis topic as suggested. I wrote Professor Rosencrass, telling him that I was interested in taking their offer. I scheduled an appointment to meet with him at Hunter as soon as the next semester commenced. I began to research members of the faculty who could advise a potential thesis. I realized that there were only four possible candidates: Professor Angelico, from whom I had taken "Historical Methods," Professor Stein, who I had for my intellectual history class, Professor Regresso, who I thought would be an excellent candidate to oversee a thesis related to Latin American history, and Professor Rosencrass because I had a relationship with him and was once again placing my future in his hands. However, any topic that related to my degree program would be outside of his area of expertise.

First, I wrote to Professor Regresso because I thought, given her expertise in Latin America, she was the leading candidate. I sent her an email in late July of 2012.

She swiftly sent me this response via Blackberry:

[Message omitted.]

I was disappointed to receive her refusal to help, particularly because she had expertise in the area I wanted to do research. I next forwarded the email to Professor Rosencrass along with my concerns and he sent me this response via Blackberry:

[Message omitted.]

I knew that I had to be careful in my preparations for meeting with potential thesis advisors in the fall, especially since I had the nagging feeling that Professor Regresso either did not grasp, or did not care to grasp what I was proposing. I also realized that I would have a better opportunity to explain my ideas in person with the other potential advisors. I needed a carefully designed plan tailored to each of the remaining professors so that I could hopefully have them want to advise my thesis.

Over the summer, while working to make a menial living in Western New York, I investigated each professor's research interests to develop a new thesis that incorporated my interest of studying Latin American themes with their areas of expertise. I looked into Professor Angelico's work, which mostly dealt with colonial U.S. history and nineteenth-century U.S. history. I researched U.S. drug policy in Latin America which I eventually pursued. I pored over thousands of pages of diverse historical materials in the weeks leading up to my meetings at Hunter scheduled for the beginning of Fall Semester 2012.

When I left for New York City, I had set up meetings with Professors Angelico and Rosencrass. I could not get a hold of Professor Rodriquez (Lehman) or Professor Stein; I would have to do my best to seek them out when I got to New York. On Tuesday, August 28, I met with Professor Rosencrass. I found out that Professor Stein was on sabbatical that semester, so he was automatically eliminated as a possible advisor. I told Professor Rosencrass that I had a meeting with Professor Angelico later in the week and if he was unable or unwilling to advise my thesis, I would be out of options. It was then that I asked Professor Rosencrass if he would be willing to be my advisor, along with Professor Rodriquez. Professor Rosencrass indicated that something could be worked out, depending on Professor Rodriquez's acceptance. I was grateful and relieved. After talking to Professor Rodriquez, who enthusiastically accepted, Professor Rosencrass also agreed to be the primary reader with Professor Rodriquez serving as the secondary.

I spent the next couple of months furiously reading up on the subject of U.S. drug policy in Latin America. I purchased dozens of books related to the topic. I arranged everything in my life so that I could stay in New York City. I started to believe that with hard work, perhaps, I might get a degree in time to gain some much needed monetary compensation by working as an adjunct professor the following fall as I had very promising leads on a couple positions at colleges near my home.

On Friday October 19, 2012, I arrived in New York just before Super Storm Sandy, which negatively impacted my plans to stay in the city. So my friend selflessly offered to let me stay with him in Connecticut indefinitely. My living arrangements, of necessity, had been changed. I worked assiduously on my thesis and in a few weeks I produced a full proposal, including an outline and preliminary bibliography, which I submitted to both professors. Then I went to work on a sample chapter at Professor Rosencrass's suggestion. The sample chapter was to be the first chapter of the thesis after the introduction. Each professor had his own philosophy on how I should proceed. Professor Rodriquez, who has always encouraged me, suggested that after submitting the sample chapter I would continue to write the thesis straight through to the end so I could have a better sense of where I was going with the project. This approach made sense to me. However, Professor Rosencrass said that the proper way to proceed would be chapter by chapter, not moving forward until he deemed each chapter to be in top shape. Since he was the primary reader and my link to finishing at Hunter, his approach prevailed.

I am sure that Professor Rosencrass felt that he was doing me a favor by agreeing to advise my thesis. However, the thesis was doomed from the onset due to the nature of the arrangement. He was meticulous about correcting each chapter to the point that the process became maddening. After approving the initial outline and bibliography, he asked me, multiple times, to change the structure, which left me feeling lost in the process and became time consuming, requiring repeated content revision. This, combined with his rigid insistence that I work with him chapter by chapter before sending a draft to Professor Rodriquez, made the process strenuous. I was forced to revise and resubmit my first chapter nine times and after a year and a half of work on my second thesis, I still found myself agonizing over it. In between submissions of my first chapter, I would work on other chapters as I awaited Professor Rosencrass's response. I had well over one hundred pages of draft. But none of this mattered until I finished the portentous first chapter. This demoralizingly critical style of Professor Rosencrass, a design in which he seems to take some pride, elicited ever decreasing confidence on my part and a dispirited, labored output. I felt abstracted from the material as I was continuously torn down but never built up. After nearly two years, Professor Rosencrass allowed me to submit my second chapter, while still working on the first. To this day, I still do not have an approved first chapter and Professor Rodriquez, the expert in the field, has not been able to read a single syllable of the thesis. Through this entire process I have been commuting back and forth to NYC for thesis meetings, incurring ever greater expenses and debts. When I last met with Professor Rosencrass, he made the completion of my degree even more difficult by deciding, at this late date, that I must find a third reader for the thesis. Moreover, he began questioning my numerous, well-researched sources (that were not in his area of expertise to begin with). I often felt like more of a nuisance than a student in my interactions with him. He did not listen to my questions, overrode my comments and became irritated if I tried to explain my perspective on the work. In my last meeting with him, he said my first chapter was "close" and that my second chapter "needed a great deal of work." I eventually became lost and frustrated in the process, feeling as if I was simply trying to please him without having the specific instruction necessary to improve the work. It became unclear to me what he wanted and the process devolved into increasingly stressful guesswork. Finally, I insisted that he read my third chapter because much of the context that I thought was missing in the second chapter would come to light and we would have a better idea of how to proceed. That conversation occurred in June. After not hearing from him for months, I wrote him on October 25, 2014, to inform him that I was quitting.

Why have I finally decided to end my relationship with Hunter College? For my entire career at your institution, the onus has always been placed on me even if the problem was institutional barriers or errors of faculty and administration. I have done everything that was asked of me and not in a mediocre way but as a 3.6 GPA student who passed a difficult comprehensive exam where I translated a document about the Ancien Regime from Spanish to English. After six years, I am completely disillusioned with Hunter and what it stands for. The experience has sapped my faith in higher education and has made me give up on my long-time desire to teach history at the college level, which I once naively thought was a passion for making a difference in people's lives. My "role models" at Hunter have demonstrated that higher education is more about building personal careers.

I believe that I have been a sincerely dedicated student. My perseverance toward the degree is exemplified by the thousands of dollars spent, resulting in stifling debt, the extensive sacrifices of travel, dedication to the material, and the fact that not even an emergency spinal cord surgery or a protracted convalescence interrupted my resolve or performance.

I believe that I have been misled by Hunter from the beginning. Faculty should have informed me that the Latin American history degree I pursued could not be fashioned, taught, or delivered. This is a matter of simple ethics. I should have been told at the outset that the listing in the catalogue was a misrepresentation and that a department in Latin American history was non-existent. Furthermore, guiding me toward a reconstituted degree in the history of U.S.-Latin American relations, even though there was a paucity of faculty and resources, resulted in an exasperatingly difficult failure. The instruction, supervision and guidance were inadequate and the delivery was, in some cases, controlling and demoralizing. The frequent inaccessibility of the faculty interrupted and protracted the work unnecessarily.

I feel it is incumbent upon Hunter to at least reimburse all my tuition and fees. I am not asking for compensation for the emotional strain and the loss of income due to required traveling to New York City periodically, nor for the thousands of dollars in other related expenses incurred during my six years of studying at Hunter College. Most importantly, I hope that my coming forth will ensure that no other student will suffer the injustices I have at the hands of your institution. I look forward to your response at your earliest convenience.

Sincerely,

Loren Mayshark

Bibliography

Capriccioso, Rob. "Hunter Settles Suicide Suit." *Inside Higher Ed* (August 24, 2006). https://www.insidehighered.com/news/2006/08/24/suicide. Accessed February 1, 2017.

Chomsky, Noam. "How America's Great University System Is Being Destroyed." Lecture, Adjunct Faculty Association of the United Steelworkers, Pittsburgh, PA. (February 4, 2014). http://www.alternet.org/corporate-accountability-and-workplace/chomsky-how-americas-great-university-system-getting. Accessed January 1, 2017.

Hunter College of the City University of New York Graduate Catalog 2006–2009. http://www.hunter.cuny.edu/onestop/repository/files/records-and-transcripts/hunter-catalog-archives/Hunter%20Graduate%20Catalog%202006-2009.pdf. Accessed February 2, 2017.

Stern, Arthur A. "When Is a Paragraph?" *College Composition and Communication*, 27: 3 (1976): 253–57. doi:10.2307/ 357044.

About the Author

Loren Mayshark was fortunate to have parents who offered him opportunities to see the world and instilled in him a passion for travel. As his wanderlust grew, he journeyed to more than thirty US states and at least as many foreign countries while visiting four continents.

After college, he supported his itinerant lifestyle by working dozens of jobs, including golf caddy, travel writer, construction worker, fireworks salesperson, substitute teacher, and vineyard laborer. Predominantly his jobs have been in the restaurant industry. He cut his teeth as a server, maître d', and bartender at San Francisco's historic Fisherman's Grotto #9, the original restaurant on the Fisherman's Wharf. While working with a colorful crew of primarily Mexican and Chinese co-workers, he gained a passion for Spanish and spent several months wandering through South America.

While living in New York City he attended both the Gotham Writers Workshop and the New York Writers Workshop. He is a regular contributor to Can the Man, an alternative media resource focused on social justice, and The Jovial Journey, a website dedicated to food, drink, and travel. He has written for The Permaculture Research Institute and Uisio among other prominent outlets.

Loren Mayshark's first book, *Death: An Exploration*, won the 2016 Beverly Hills Book Award in the category of Death and Dying and is a finalist for book of the year in the 2016 Foreword INDIES

Awards in the category of Grief/Grieving (Adult Nonfiction).

He received a BA in World History from Manhattanville College in 2004 while minoring in World Religions. He attended the MA History program at Hunter College in Manhattan.

For more information visit his website: lorenmayshark.com.

Red Scorpion Press was formed in January 2016 with the hope of bettering the world in a small way through publishing. Our aim is to push boundaries and be an outlet for fresh voices and unique perspectives that entertain and inform.

Please visit us at www.redscorpionpress.com for our latest selection of books.

www.ingramcontent.com/pod-product-compliance
Lightning Source LLC
Chambersburg PA
CBHW020616300426
44113CB00007B/672